Building Blocks

for Performance

Bobbie Anderson
with Tracy Libby

Alpine
Blue Ribbon Books
Loveland, Colorado

Building Blocks for Performance
Copyright ©2002 Bobbie Anderson and Tracy Libby

Library of Congress Cataloging-in-Publication Data

Anderson Bobbie, 1936-
    Building blocks for performance / Bobbie Anderson ; written by Tracy Libby.
       p. cm.
    Includes bibliographical references and index.
    ISBN 1-57779-037-5
       1. Field trials. 2. Puppies--Training. 3. Dogs--Training. I. Libby, Tracy, 1958- II. Title.

SF425.5.A542002
636.7'0835--dc21
2002025403

This book is available at special quantity discounts for breeders and for club promotions, premiums, or educational use. Write for details.

The information contained in this book is complete and accurate to the best of our knowledge. All recommendations are made without guarantee on the part of the author or Alpine Publications, Inc. The author and publisher disclaim any liability with the use of this information.

Designed by: Laura Claassen

Photos by Tracy Libby unless otherwise credited

Front Cover Photos: (top) Weimaraner Ch. Zara N Nambé's One In A Zillion, CD, as a puppy, owned and photographed by Meredith John; (center) Trinity Craigmour Taz'll Do, MX, MXJ, TD, CDX, VCD-II, HIAs, owned by Sandra Schmidt and Jean Clodwick and photographed by Anita Paull; (bottom left) Puppy owned by Tammy Burkett, Agility Dream, and photographed by Mark Gose; (bottom right) Bobbie Anderson and Redtop Jag, photographed by Tracy Libby.

First printing: April 2002

  2 3 4 5 6 7 8 9 0

Printed in the United States of America.

Table of Contents

Foreword

Twelve years ago when I met Bobbie Anderson, I immediately realized that she had something very special with her dogs. She had developed the type of relationship with them that many handlers strive for yet seldom achieve. What separates Bobbie from the majority of handlers is that her dogs idolize her; they want to work for her. The trust and respect between her and her dogs provide the fundamental base for successful competition. As a result, all her dogs—regardless of breed—possess a keenness, enthusiasm, and an intense desire to work. This is what I refer to as "the want."

Over the years I have developed a true friendship with Bobbie. She has done a magnificent job with her dogs, successfully incorporating many elements of my "It's Magic" style of training into her own. As a trainer Bobbie is generous with her knowledge, truly encouraging and assisting other handlers to succeed with their dogs.

This book shares Bobbie's training philosophy. It takes the reader step-by-step through her basic procedures of utilizing play in training to develop the human/canine relationship which Bobbie feels is essential for today's competitive canine environment.

While the focus of this book is on raising and training a puppy for performance, anyone with the desire to train a dog will find in these pages a unique approach to the art of puppy training. A handler using the philosophy and ideas expressed in this book will be well on the way to developing the type of human/canine relationship that fosters enthusiasm and desire to work in their puppy.

Sylvia Bishop
England, 2001

Sylvia Bishop is recognized as England's top obedience handler and trainer. She is known around the world as one of the foremost authorities on canine training, competition, and behavior. Her prestigious records include: qualifying for Crufts twenty-eight years in a row, finishing eight champions, over one hundred championship wins, and a record number of multiple dogs at Crufts. Her expertise as an instructor is in constant demand. She has conducted training seminars throughout England, the United States, Canada, New Zealand, and Europe.

Acknowledgments

I am indebted to many people for the knowledge and inspiration I have gained over the past thirty years. A special thank you to Sylvia Bishop, whose friendship, encouragement, motivation, and tutelage have afforded me the opportunity to refine and strengthen my ideas about dog training. Her expertise and phenomenal insight elevated the human/canine relationship to a new level and revolutionized the training techniques of countless handlers and trainers.

Jack Godsil, Marly Whiting, Diane Bauman, Patty Ruzzo, and Andrea Vaughan have all had a significant and lasting influence on my training over the years.

Thanks, too, to all my wonderful Shelties—Sparkle, Bronco, Jiffy, Caper, and Cajun—and to my German Shepherd, English Cockers, and remarkable Border Collies. Each dog has challenged and inspired me to become a more informed and creative trainer.

I am indebted to the many hundreds of students whose enduring affection for their dogs has been a constant source of incentive and encouragement. They have provided me with an invaluable education.

Finally, a special thank you to my husband, Rolf, for never complaining about the dogs.

Bobbie Anderson

A special thanks to my husband, Paul, whose love and encouragement have been the constant in my life, enabling me the opportunity to write and train dogs every day.

To my parents who have loved me through all of my endeavors—canine or otherwise. Thanks for never saying no when I brought home another dog.

To Bobbie Anderson for her expertise, patience, friendship, and tutelage over the years. To Sylvia Bishop for generously sharing her knowledge as well as her kindness and words of wisdom through the years. To my dear friend Michelle Hall for her proof reading, her friendship when others wavered, and for loving the dogs. To the staff of Alpine Publications for their expertise and guidance, and to Diane Bauman for her insight.

Finally, to all the dogs, past and present, that have touched my life and who are the source and inspiration for this book. I live in gratitude to each and every one.

Tracy J. Libby

Introduction

There are many wonderful methods for training puppies. My goal with this book is to offer you training methods and techniques that will help you to build a solid foundation of behaviors in your future performance dog. While the methods in this book will work with any dog, they are designed especially for owners and handlers who intend to raise and train a puppy for competition in obedience, herding, agility, tracking, lure coursing, flyball, or any other competitive performance events. The methods I will teach you apply to puppies from six weeks to one year of age. In this book I assume that training begins when the puppy goes to a new home at eight or nine weeks of age. Behaviors are shaped by repetition and by building each lesson on the previous one, step-by-step. Whether you start with a puppy that is eight weeks or five months of age, the same principles apply. The length of time a puppy trains will vary depending on his temperament, energy level and so forth. A training session for an eight or ten-week-old puppy may be two or three minutes several times a day. A five- or six-month-old puppy can usually work for ten or fifteen minutes once or twice a day.

First, you will learn how to build a trusting relationship with your puppy. Second, you will learn how to instill enthusiasm, motivation, and an unwavering desire to work.

Training dogs for competition is a journey that can be simultaneously exhilarating and exasperating. Fortunately, good dog trainers, like good cooks, can learn by imitating their peers. When given the proper ingredients and guidelines, almost any sound puppy can grow into an adult dog that is capable of some level of competitive success. My hope is that this book will help you succeed in these events by improving your training techniques. Most of all, I hope to make training and showing fun for both you and your puppy. If there is no joy in training and showing—what's the point?

Within these pages you will find a combination of philosophy and training techniques that I have accumulated during my thirty years of training dogs. This ideology has helped me to put over seventy AKC titles on dogs, including five OTCHs, and more than eighty-five High in Trials. As you read you will no doubt come across some ideas that you absolutely love, and others that seem questionable or downright nutty. That's okay. As you build your own mosaic of knowledge, it will be your job as a trainer to sort through the myriad of training techniques and pick those that work successfully for you and your puppy.

I invite you to read, apply, and test the ideas and techniques presented. Choose those that work for your individual puppy, and remember, no two puppies react alike. Come on, let's get started building that future winner!

Bobbie Anderson
January 2002

Why Puppies Do What They Do

IN TODAY'S COMPETITIVE ENVIRONMENT it seems there are as many trainers and training methods as there are breeds of dogs. These methods include positive and negative motivation, food training, play training, toy training, and clicker training. Throw in the endless variety of paraphernalia employed, from electronic gizmos to metallic gadgetry, and the entire process can seem more complicated than computer science.

Performance dog handlers want a dog with an unrelenting attitude and a "Send me in, coach!" spirit. They want a dog that is fast, enthusiastic, motivated, confident, and eager to perform on any turf—grass, dirt, water, or a muddy field thick enough to suck your boots off. How many times have you seen a dog performing with speed, enthusiasm, and acuity and said to yourself, "My next dog will work like that"?

The good news is this is an achievable and realistic goal. In dog training, as in anything else in life, you cannot expect something for nothing. Competition is fierce at the elite level. In fact, the sport of dogs is one of the few venues where amateurs and professionals compete side-by-side for the same points, legs, and rosettes. The professionals—those individuals who make money training and handling dogs—have dedicated their lives to the sport. In addition to having spent years apprenticing, they continue to spend countless hours every day, 365 days a year, honing their craft. They are counting on the blue ribbons to enhance their careers and reputations. They are your competition.

Puppy training the future performance dog takes smart management, good dogmanship, an enduring love of the sport, an endless reserve of patience, an ample supply of common sense, and creativity. You will need the ability to view setbacks with a healthy sense of humor. In fact, some days a sense of humor will be the only thing that keeps you from plunging head first into complete lunacy. There are no money-back guarantees in the sport of dogs. It is hard work training and competing successfully, but it is not impossible. On any given weekend and at any given show or trial, it is all up for grabs. When you and your dog come out on top, the heartache and disappointment of previous shows will be nothing more than a distant memory. Well, at least for a day or two!

Labradors instinctively love water and retrieving. These are inherited characteristics of the breed. Photo © Robert and Eunice Pearcy.

THE GENETIC LOTTERY

There are countless books and research studies available that do an excellent job of deciphering the intricacies of genetics and animal behavior. Most are based on the works of Charles Darwin, Gregor Johann Mendel, Konrad Lorenz and Drs. John L. Fuller and John Paul Scott, to name a few. Genetics is a comprehensive and exhaustive topic that goes well beyond the scope of this book. Yet, without delving too deeply into the complexities of the subject, it is safe to say that dogs do what they do for two reasons: 1) inherited characteristics, and 2) acquired behaviors. Inherited characteristics—also

Attempting to suppress or eradicate a herding dog's passion to herd or a terrier's quest to dig is fruitless. On the other hand, trying to establish behaviors that are not endemic to a particular breed, such as expecting a Border Collie to guard sheep or a Saint Bernard to possess the upbeat temperament of a Bichon Frise, will only make your competitive career, not to mention your life, miserable.

A Border Collie is born to herd.

known as genetic predispositions—are the traits that Mother Nature genetically preprograms. These traits are pretty much guaranteed to appear later on in your puppy's life whether you want them to or not. Some examples include the running ability of Greyhounds, the pulling and running tendencies of sled dogs, the digging behavior of terriers, and the stalking, chasing, and nipping actions of herding dogs.

These natural tendencies and characteristics are part of the puppy's complete package.

Here is where trainers often run afoul. They attempt to lump their own feelings, values, and desires onto their puppy. They fail to take into account that every puppy, first and foremost, is an individual. He will not automatically love to train and show just because he is a Golden Retriever. Many handlers want their puppy—regardless of his breed—to grow into an adult dog that works with the speed and acuity of a Border Collie. The majority of Basenjis will never possess the natural retrieving instincts of a Border Collie. Basenjis are Basenjis—they are not and never will be Border Collies. Most Basenjis are not motivated by toys. Where retrieving is concerned, they think that if you want something picked up you should do it yourself. This does not mean that a Basenji is not fun, enthusiastic and eager to work. However, it behooves you to recognize your puppy's inherited predispositions and build upon them rather than expend valuable energy trying to establish behaviors that are not endemic to your breed or individual puppy.

Genetic predispositions should not be used as an excuse for allowing sloppy habits such as boredom, lack of attention, slow recalls or retrieves, or sloppy sits to creep into your training program. If you have created a problem, it is your job as a trainer to go back and fix it. Do not ignore the problem or shrug it off as a behavior that is indigenous to your puppy. If, on the other hand, you put a Utility Dog Excellent title on a Shar Pei or a Masters Agility title on a Basset Hound then you have definitely earned bragging rights.

Acquired behaviors are exactly what the name implies—behaviors your puppy acquired from the day he was born. These behaviors are learned—be they good or bad, desired or undesired. When puppies are tiny, their mother licks and nudges and rolls them as a form of teaching. If the occasion war-

A puppy that learns enthusiasm and desire through fun and games will grow into an adult dog with enthusiasm and desire. Photo © Robert and Eunice Pearcy.

rants, she might growl or nip as a form of communication and discipline. As the puppies mature both physically and mentally, her actions become more forceful. She tells them in no uncertain terms which behaviors are acceptable and which are not.

If you call your six-month-old Golden Retriever and he comes tearing over to you with his head and ears up, his tail wagging and a happy attitude that screams, "What are we going to do now?" that is an acquired behavior. If, on the other hand, that same puppy chooses to ignore you and decides instead to tend to some urgent puppy business such as chasing a squirrel, sniffing some grass or exploring a pile of leaves, that, too, is an acquired behavior. Somewhere along the line the puppy has learned that to ignore you is acceptable.

INDIVIDUAL PERSONALITY

Life would be easier if there were a definite formula for raising and training puppies. However, just like children, puppies must be raised as individuals if you want to make the most of their personalities and talents. Weimaraner puppies, for example, look strikingly similar in appearance, will track their owner

A litter of seven-week-old Siberian Huskies. Each one will have his own distinctive personality. Photo by Karen Damoth Yeargain.

all over the house and yard, and can pass a Tracking Dog test with ease. However, despite their littermate status and uniform physical appearance, each puppy will develop into a unique individual with his own distinct spirit, personality, and genetic makeup. As a result of this genetic lottery, plus some environmental influences, each puppy will react differently to social situations and training techniques.

It is important that you understand your puppy's breed, history, and origin. I firmly believe that before you start training any puppy you should commit to memory his breed's standard. You should understand the soul and essence of the breed. At the very least, you should understand its original function

and purpose, country of origin, and why that particular breed was developed. Armed with this information you are better equipped to understand and deal with your puppy's specific behaviors.

Furthermore, it helps to have some basic knowledge of the dog's pedigree, his sire, dam and littermates. However, the most significant information will come from learning your puppy's temperament and personality, his quirks and idiosyncrasies, and how and why he reacts to various situations. Simply put, you need to find out what makes him tick. Remember those inherited predispositions? Get in the habit of really watching and observing your puppy at every opportunity. The knowledge you gain will be indispensable. Plus, it's free! Congress hasn't yet figured out how to tax it, license, copyright or outlaw it, so use it to your advantage!

Watch your puppy when he's sleeping, playing by himself, or with other dogs, cats, or with children. Is your puppy bold? Timid? Does he charge into a room full of energy and self-confidence? Or, like his owner, does he need a double latte before he will even consider retrieving? Is he pushy? Bossy? Aggressive? Sassy? Does he have ants in his pants? What's his peak energy time? How does he react in hot weather, cold weather, and unfamiliar surroundings? Does he hold a grudge? Is he inquisitive or curious? Does he wag his tail and spring to life when he sees you? Does he have a great desire to please you, or could he care less about you and your bucket full of toys? Are you doing all the work while he whimpers, "Must I wag my tail today?"

You can wave a dog's blue ribbon pedigree about all you want, but the behaviors you should be most concerned about are the behaviors that he *personally* displays. These are the only behaviors that you can be absolutely, positively sure apply to him. Once you have

Part of the socialization period should include exposing your puppy to a variety of sights, sounds, smells, and other animals. Always do so in a controlled and safe environment. Photo © Robert and Eunice Pearcy.

a keen sense of his personality you can design a training program that utilizes his specific traits to encourage desired behaviors and discourage unwanted ones.

For instance, Shelties are notorious for barking. They were originally bred as an all-purpose dog that would alert farmers to intruders. Their barking is part and parcel of their breeding. Knowing this ahead of time, you can encourage or discourage the behavior depending upon your preferences.

Some breeds, including Shelties, are prone to spookiness. Knowing this, you can design a socialization program that builds confidence in your puppy. It might include taking him to work with you, for rides in the car and walks in the park, and to puppy socialization classes, as well as supervised contact with other puppies, with cats, horses, sheep, kids, and women in floppy hats. You might encourage friends or visitors to get on the ground and talk to him, play with him, rub his tummy, and kiss his nose. Try exposing him, in a positive environment, to the show scene by taking him to obedience, conformation or agility shows, herding trials, or track-

Observe how your puppy reacts around other animals and in strange surroundings.

ing events. Take him for a walk around the show grounds or keep him safely confined in an exercise pen as he experiences the sights, sounds, and smells of his future career.

If your puppy is pushy and bossy, from day one you should discourage the behavior of grabbing toys or food out

Introduce your puppy to a variety of places including water, rocks, gravel, and lawns. Always do so in a safe and controlled environment. Photo © Robert and Eunice Pearcy.

of your hand without permission. If you want a fast puppy, encourage speed by never slowing him down. If your puppy has an upbeat, playful attitude, foster and encourage it by acting upbeat and fun yourself.

If you establish mutual respect early in the human/canine relationship, obedience training will be merely a matter of shaping and channeling specific behaviors. For instance, if your daily walks with your puppy are fun and interactive and if pulling on the leash is not an issue, then you won't need a pinch collar to teach heeling. If a puppy learns to "wait" and not bolt out the door, then teaching the stay command becomes a piece of cake. If you have played interactive games such as hiding toys and cookies around the house and then helping your puppy "find it," scent discrimination will become more understandable and easier to teach your puppy.

There are few perfect puppies—despite our personal (and often biased) opinions. One trick of good training is to recognize which behaviors (including faults) you can live with and which might preclude a long and useful show career.

THE PUPPY'S WORLDVIEW

A puppy's brain is not hardwired to be vindictive or vengeful. Despite what some owners think, puppies do not understand disobedience or anti-social behavior. They don't wake up in the morning and ponder antagonistic thoughts such as, "I'm not going to herd today because my owner didn't play ball with me." Nor do they contemplate how to single-handedly destroy an expensive Italian leather sofa because their owner left them at home alone. Dogs live in the present. They tend to do exactly what pleases them at any given moment unless someone is directing them otherwise. Puppies react

Decide early on which behaviors you will or will not accept.

A puppy's natural curiosity can get him into trouble. Puppies should learn early on not to chase cats or other animals.

to stimuli and specific situations; they don't sit around thinking about their indiscretions or watching *Oprah* to find out how they should respond to a particular situation.

If your six-month-old puppy does the belly crawl across the room when you arrive home and discover he has gnawed the leg off your antique Duncan-Phyfe chair, it is not because he has any comprehension of his dastardly deed. He is reacting to your mannerisms and tone of voice. You might not realize it, but your facial expressions at that moment probably resemble an unmade bed. Your jaw might be clenched, your breathing labored, and your body posture threatening. Puppies have remarkable powers of observation and possess the uncanny ability to zero in on even the slightest changes in body language. The stronger the bond your puppy develops with you, the more in tune he will be to subtle changes in your deportment.

Old or young, dogs do not have the mental wherewithal to make the connection between their actions ten minutes or two hours ago and your current

A ten-week old Australian Shepherd contemplates the rules of the game.

disposition. If he perceives that you are angry, your dog will think you are angry simply because you arrived home. This is a difficult concept for handlers to grasp. They want to believe that their puppy has committed a heinous crime out of spite and his submissive behavior is the result of being apprehended.

Handlers have the same preconceived notions when their dog blows his

7

sit-stay in the obedience ring, throws a tizzy in the breed ring, or ignores a "down" command in the field. "He knows exactly what he's done," handlers will protest. "Look at him. He even has a guilty look on his face." Or, my personal favorite, "He broke his sit-stay to get even with me." Get over it!

What pleases puppies often annoys owners. Puppies love to dig in the dirt. If they happen to dig up $200 worth of tulip bulbs in the process—oh well—that was not their intention. If a cat runs they chase it, and they are prepared to chase it a good long way. Your puppy cannot perceive that you are already twenty minutes late for work. If a puppy relieves himself on your expensive Oriental rug, it is safe to say he had a full bladder at that moment and you weren't paying enough attention to notice. Ninety-nine percent of all canine training and behavior problems occur because owners fail to correctly recognize and analyze the situation and subsequently change the pattern of canine responses.

In this book, I hope to teach you to be more aware of your puppy, to utilize his or her innate abilities, and to shape the behavior you want right from the start. These are important concepts when training any puppy, but they become especially significant when you want that puppy to be your next performance champion. Think of them as building blocks that help prepare your puppy for competition, and now let's get started.

Some puppies are born with an insatiable desire to play. Learn to foster and capitalize on that behavior.

Block One: Build A Strong Relationship

No doubt about it, puppies are irresistible. They are cute, cuddly, enticing bundles of fur, but do not let their looks deceive you. They also learn to be manipulative at an early age. A sad, pitiful look usually gets them a tidbit of food from the table. It is then a short leap from pitiful look to seasoned con artist. Before you know it your precious angel is stealing food off the counters, ignoring commands, and committing heinous crimes against your personal property. If your relatives behaved like that, you would disown them.

Fast-forward two years. You walk into an obedience or agility ring and your dog breaks his "down," ever so slightly curls his lip at the judge, or snarls at another dog. Perhaps your herding dog chooses to ignore an "away to me" or "lie down" command. Unfortunately, many handlers fail to make the connection between the tyrant that commits unspeakable acts against their personal property and the same dog that refuses to obey his handler's commands, lacks respect both in and out of the ring, and repeatedly turns in a poor performance.

Puppies are cute and cuddly, but don't let looks deceive you. It's a short leap from cute and cuddly to seasoned con artist. Photo by Sandy Mortensen.

A puppy that learns to respect his owner on a day-to-day basis will grow into an adult dog that respects his owner in a competitive or working environment.

SCHOOL IS ALWAYS IN SESSION

Regardless of your chosen field of competition, laying the groundwork for a successful working relationship with your puppy as he grows and matures requires more than a fifteen-minute training session each day. A successful relationship in the competition ring is dependent on the twenty-four-hour-a-day relationship between the handler and the dog. It is built on a solid foundation of mutual respect, trust, patience, understanding, acceptance, fairness, consistency, and love. Respect stems from the communication and interaction between you and the puppy on a daily basis, whether you are in the kitchen, in the car, at a show or in the training building. The cardinal rule of dog training is that you should consider every moment spent with your puppy as a training session. Every time you are with your puppy you are instilling either desired or undesired behaviors. School is always in session. The behav-

Consider every moment you spend with your puppy a training session.

iors you decide to accept or reject are your decision.

Simply put, your success in the ring will come from the relationship you have established with your puppy as he grows and matures into an adult dog. Puppies grow into adult dogs that are a direct reflection of what you have put into them. I tell my students all the time, "Every handler gets the dog they deserve." If you are happy, fun, and upbeat, your puppy will absorb the same attitude and become an adult dog that is happy and upbeat. If you are as dull as a post, he, too, will be dull.

Furthermore, if your puppy is allowed to cultivate rude and disrespectful habits such as bolting through doors, stealing food, running away, or randomly ignoring you, you can never hope to have success for three minutes in the ring. How can you expect a puppy to grow into an adult dog that comes quickly and enthusiastically in competition when he is not required to do so on a daily basis at home? How can you expect your herding dog

With the help of a longline or Flexi™ the handler maintains control of the situation, thereby denying the puppy the opportunity to wander off and/or ignore his owner.

to down immediately in the field when he is not required to obey the down command in your living room? Sniffing, inattention, boredom, and disrespect outside the ring lead to the same behaviors inside the ring. Handlers need to think about that concept.

Let's say, for example, you are playing with your twelve-week-old puppy and working on the sit command. Your future performance dog, however, decides a pile of leaves or a patch of weeds is more exciting than you. Rather than allow him to ignore you, do something silly to get his attention back on you. He must learn (in a fun manner) that you will not allow him to develop the habit of tuning you out. You can gently poke or tweak him and say "I got you!" When he looks at you, praise him for looking. "Aren't you clever!" or "Good boy!"

If you are working on some fun puppy recall games and he decides to chase after a bird, wander over to his water bowl or lie down on the grass, you must do silly things to get his attention back on you. Try falling on the ground and rolling around or banging his toy on the side of a building. You

must do something to create in him the desire to come running back to you. Praise him lavishly when he gets to you. Avoid making a habit of going and getting your puppy. Instead, do something loony and laughable to make him want to come back to you.

A longline is essential. Whenever I am out with my puppy, I always attach a longline to his buckle collar so that I can maintain control of the situation. He is never given the opportunity to wander or run away from me. If for some reason he even starts to wander off, all I need to do is step on the longline. I say to him, "I've got you!" and I do something to make him want to come running back. If necessary, I will reel him back in using the longline.

From day one it is essential that you do not allow your puppy to develop the bad habit of ignoring you. If he learns to ignore you when he is young, he will most definitely ignore you when he is an adult. If your dog already has developed the nasty habit of ignoring, you have two choices. You can go back to the basics and begin the long and often arduous task of retraining him to focus on you. Or you can get out of dogs and take up bowling because your chances of success in any arena of canine competition are slim to none.

RESPECT IS THE BOTTOM LINE

Puppies do not live in or comprehend a democratic society where voting determines who gets to eat first, hunt, breed, or get the cushiest spot for sleeping. Long before dogs were domesticated they lived in packs where their

"Are you talking to me?" At four months of age puppies begin to test you to see if they must obey.

survival depended upon their ability to cooperate and coexist. A dog's individual personality and pack status were integral in maintaining continuity within the pack. For instance, if all the dogs had alpha, top dog, or leadership type personalities the result would be constant bickering, infighting and challenging. The pack would never survive. It would lack a single, clear leader. On the other hand, if all the dogs were submissive the pack would lack the leadership necessary for survival. None of the dogs would take charge. To coexist peacefully

and guarantee their survival, the pack must have a clearly defined chain of command. It is this pack instinct, or hierarchical system, that allows dogs to respect and revere a strong clear leader. *In a domesticated environment that leader must be you.*

It is this preprogrammed behavior of submission to and appeasement of higher ranking animals that allows a domesticated dog to accept you as his leader. Therefore, it is essential that you establish yourself, in a fun and humane manner, as the alpha, or "top dog," early on in the human/canine relationship.

If your puppy learns to respect you at an early age he will respect you when he is two, five and nine years old. Ideally, if you raise a puppy or get one eight weeks old, by the time he is three-and-one-half or four months old he should have developed the foundation of respecting you. That is, provided you have laid the proper groundwork and instilled the behaviors that build a solid and mutually respectable human/canine relationship.

A puppy eight to twelve weeks of age generally will follow you everywhere. His mother and siblings are gone. You are his security. By fourteen or fifteen weeks, the puppy has been out and about socializing and exploring his new surroundings. He is more confident and secure and doesn't need you quite as much as he did earlier. This is the age most puppies will test their owner. Here is a typical scenario: the four-month-old puppy is doing something interesting, such as sniffing a leaf or exploring a flower. You call, "Puppy, come!" as you take off running to incite his chase instinct, but he decides he doesn't need you anymore so he ignores you. He is testing you to see if he really has to come when called. *This is a critical junction in the human/canine relationship—the point where you establish in your puppy's mind who is the boss.* If you ignore him and allow him to go about his

A mother dog rarely under- or over-corrects her puppies. Photo by Karen Damoth Yeargain.

business, or give him multiple requests to come, you are allowing him to make choices. If allowed to make choices in his day-to-day life, he will learn to make choices in a competitive environment. One day he will choose not to heel, come, down, jump, retrieve (or whatever the command). Therefore, it is important that you not let him ignore you. Give him a little shake on his collar, "Hey, I said come." Or, give him a little tweak on his hind end to get his attention. This is the point where you reinforce in your puppy's mind that *you* are top dog—not him. This type of early and consistent attention to specific behaviors will carry over into your training program and eventually into the ring.

If, however, the puppy looks to you for leadership and sees none, he is no doubt cocky enough and more than willing to accept the job opening and appoint himself top dog. He will acquire his own rules and code of conduct and he will do as he pleases when he pleases regardless of your expectations or concerns. This will create nothing but misery in your life when it comes to living, training, and competing with the dog.

You have probably observed the scenario at shows or training seminars where the handler is doing all the work while the dog gives nothing in return. An adult dog that has never learned to respect his owner will put forth just enough energy to barely comply. Moreover, he will show his complete and utter disrespect by stopping midpoint to sniff the ground, hike his leg, or sashay nonchalantly out of the training building. This same dog is constantly bucking for a promotion by snarling, growling or snapping at his owner because he does not feel like doing the command that is asked of him.

If a puppy never learns to respect you, and subsequently feels like giving you nothing, then that's exactly what you will get from him in competition—absolutely nothing. Teaching your puppy to respect you is smart dog management with a good dose of common sense.

Let's say your five-month-old future performance star is happily retrieving a ball when he suddenly shoves his nose inside your training bag and rudely scarfs down a bag of hot dogs treats. In a pack situation a subordinate dog would not dare display such blatantly disrespectful behavior—death would be a very real consequence. In a human/canine relationship, where you are considered the pack leader, your puppy must also learn that this type of disrespectful behavior is not acceptable. Unfortunately, more often than not, handlers dismiss such behavior as just puppy antics. By ignoring the situation, they inadvertently start the puppy down the dead-end road of disrespect. Just as you would not allow a small child to arbitrarily snatch food off another family member's plate, or to steal toys from a sibling, you must not permit a puppy to develop disrespectful habits on a daily basis.

Ideally, you should ask the puppy to "give" or "drop" the stolen item. If he refuses, physically remove it from his

DOOR-BOLTING

One solution I picked up from Sylvia Bishop years ago that has worked successfully for me is to attach a longline to the puppy's collar. When the puppy bolts out a door, simply close the door behind him. The longline will catch in the door and prevent him from going anywhere. Wait ten or fifteen seconds before opening the door with much surprise. "What are you doing out there, you silly boy?" Usually it takes only a few episodes before the puppy learns that bolting out the door will not buy him anything. As your puppy matures and learns the "wait" or "stay" command, simply tell him to wait while you walk through the doorway first.

mouth. (If the puppy snarls or threatens, this becomes an entirely different issue that must be addressed immediately.) Once the stolen food has been repossessed, put the puppy on a leash and tell him "Leave it," as you toss the food a foot or so in front of him. If he lunges for it, which more than likely he will do, give him a quick pop on his nose and tell him "Leave it" or "No." When he stops lunging for the food, praise him with "Good boy!" You can then pick the food up and give it to him as a reward.

The same concept applies to puppies that are allowed to cultivate the rude habit of bolting out doors, running off, or refusing to come when called. These are sterling examples of canine disrespect. For example, your four-month-old puppy mistakenly thinks it's his job to barge past you and beat you out the door each and every time it's opened. Unless you deal with the situation immediately by teaching your puppy to behave like a gentleman and to "wait" until you go through the door first, your puppy will never learn to respect you. If he does not respect you around the house, he will not magically respect you in a competitive environment.

TIME IS OF THE ESSENCE

A sound working relationship begins the moment your new puppy arrives at your home. There is much to accomplish and a very small window of opportunity, so it's important to use your time wisely.

Students will sometimes say to me, "I've got a ten-week-old puppy but I'm going out of town for a few weeks so I'll bring him back to puppy class in two or three weeks." A ten-week-old puppy is ten weeks old for exactly seven days. There are socialization skills a puppy must learn between eight and sixteen weeks of age. *Once that small window of opportunity has passed, it can never be recaptured.*

You should be socializing, fostering desired behaviors, and laying a positive foundation during this period. This will help the puppy develop the socialization skills and coping mechanisms necessary to grow into a mentally sound and confident adult dog. You should teach the puppy to accept being handled and groomed. He should be exposed, in a positive environment, to the clapping of hands, the jiggling of car keys, the clatter of dog bowls. He should explore a variety of surfaces such as stairs, grass, cement walkways, or gravel driveways. Allow him to investigate trees, branches, leaves, insects, and other animal odors. You should *never* coddle or otherwise reward a puppy that shows fear—that only reinforces his fear. Praise him for being brave and inquisitive with "Good smelling!" or "Good find!"

Enlarge the puppy's world by exposing him to the scents, sounds, behaviors, and equipment he will encounter in his competitive career. You can expose a herding puppy to sheep or ducks in a small, controlled environment. Expose your obedience puppy to dumbbells, articles, gloves, jump sticks, and so forth. Let your future performance puppy play in and around boxes, buckets or tunnels.

As you can see, there is plenty of work to accomplish in an eight-week period. That is why you must use your time wisely. If deprived of these experiences during this specific time period, the puppy can develop fearful reactions to people, noise, or situations. By six months of age the puppy raised with limited opportunities for socialization and play has reached the point where reconditioning him is difficult, if not impossible. He will never grow into the dog he could have been if the owner had properly socialized him during this critical period.

There are many instances when handlers—for whatever reason—obtain a puppy five or six months old or older. My Sheltie, Connor, was sixteen months old when I brought him home. My English Cocker, Banjo, was seven months old, and Denver, another English Cocker, was eleven weeks old. I was able to form strong and lasting relationships with these dogs. They all competed successfully in competitive events. However, I believe they would have been more competitive if I could have maximized their socialization and training during the critical period.

Photo courtesy of Bobby Anderson.

Photo by Meredith John.

Enlarge your puppy's world by exposing him to the atmosphere, scents, and sounds that he will encounter later in competition. Photo courtesy of Diane Bauman.

15

Teach your puppy to learn and enjoy learning. A puppy has a short attention span, so quit while he is still craving more. Photo courtesy of Diane Bauman.

My goals for puppy training are to instill attitude and enthusiasm, and to teach the puppy how to learn and enjoy learning. I always train for attitude over precision, because without attitude you have nothing on which to build. Later on I will focus on how much precision he is capable of giving me. Attitude is very important. I never was willing to sacrifice attitude for precision. Therefore, I had to find a way to make them both work together.

From the time you bring your puppy home, or from the time he is eight weeks old if you raised him, your behaviors and your actions, if done correctly, establish a sound and confident relationship. Your puppy will come to believe that you are the most exciting aspect of his world, and he will learn to trust you completely. He will learn that you will not arbitrarily correct him for something he does not understand or has not yet learned. As he grows and matures and your relationship flourishes, he must trust you 100 percent. When he is sent on a go-out, across a dog walk or over a high jump, he must know that it is safe. Likewise, when he is asked to do a sit-stay while you leave the obedience ring, he must believe completely that it is safe and that you will always return to him.

Between 8 and 16 weeks of age is a critical period for socialization.

BONDING

One of the most important and essential aspects of building a solid relationship is teaching your puppy to bond with you rather than with other dogs or toys. *In order to be successful in any competitive canine event, you must be the center of your dog's universe.* You must be ground zero for his fun. If a puppy or adult dog is allowed to wander off and play with his favorite toy anytime his little heart desires, why does he need you? If he is allowed to play with other puppies whenever he feels like it, why does he need you? If he can create his own fun whenever and wherever he wants, why does he need you? Get the picture?

Personally, I would be devastated if my puppy thought playing with other dogs or toys was more exciting than playing with me. I want his major source of fun to be playing with me.

Interactive play helps build a strong human/canine relationship. Photo by Lana Young Photography.

Kisses are free! Tracy Libby with her ten-week-old Australian Shepherd. Photo by Paul Libby.

Therefore, I work hard at establishing myself as the most exciting aspect of my puppy's world.

First, I keep him with me almost constantly when he is a young puppy. For the first four to six months of his life I handle him at every opportunity. I play with him, snuggle with him, kiss his nose and revel in his puppy breath. I take him for walks to the park and rides in the car. I brush him, feed him, love him, and talk to him. I take him to herding trials, obedience shows, tracking events. I expose him to the sights and smells he will encounter as an adult in his competitive career. Not only am I cultivating his zany spirit, I am instilling the behavior of bonding with me rather than with other dogs or toys.

Second, I teach him early on that everything we do together—training,

Handle your puppy at every opportunity. Play with him, snuggle him, kiss his nose and revel in his puppy breath.

Give your puppy a toy when you have to leave him alone. Photo by Sandy Mortensen.

playing, grooming, riding in the car, or going for a walk—is going to be fun and exciting.

If a puppy is housed in a kennel or dog yard with other dogs for eight or ten hours a day, he will bond with them rather than you. This is such a fundamental element of raising and training a future competition dog that it bears repeating. The other dogs will become the number one influence and companions to your puppy. Hence, he will have little or no desire to please you. His allegiance will be to the other dogs and to his toys. No humans need apply.

I know you are probably thinking, "What about those of us who work full-time and cannot spend twenty-four hours a day with our puppy?" You can still teach your puppy to bond with you by housing him alone in a kennel run with a chew toy or bone while you are at work. After work, you are no doubt exhausted and would much prefer to curl up in a recliner and watch television. However, if you want a successful competition dog two or three years down the road, you must motivate yourself to

YOU must become the center of your dog's world!

invest quality time during your puppy's formative period. The time you commit to bonding with him, talking to him, loving him, snuggling with him, and training him is well worth it. It does require a solid commitment of time and effort.

How much time is required for bonding? It really depends on the puppy. Each one is unique and individual and must be treated as such. For instance, herding, working, and sporting dogs were originally bred to work closely with man and therefore bond with their owners quite quickly. Generally, it takes about fifteen minutes for my Border Collies, Shelties, and German Shepherds to bond with me. Nevertheless, I keep them with me almost constantly for four to six months in order to cement a lasting commitment. Hounds and terriers, on the other hand, are very independent. Making yourself the center of their universe will take some doing.

To be successful in accomplishing a solid bond with your dog, you must work at it every day. The time you spend bonding, socializing and building a solid relationship with your puppy during his formative period will greatly reduce your workload as he matures and begins to endure the rigors of training and campaigning.

LIMITED ACCESS

For the first four to six months I do not allow a new puppy free access to the dog yard or kennels where my other dogs are running, playing or sleeping. The key word, of course, is "free" access. When I am in the dog yard cleaning up or puttering about he is allowed to run, play, romp and socialize with my other dogs for as long as I am in the dog yard. When I leave, he leaves with me. He is never left unattended with my other dogs.

While I train my other dogs, he is confined in his crate or a kennel. On rare occasions I allow him to run and play in the training building as a distraction while I train one of my other dogs. I do this sparingly, however. When the puppy is in the building it is impossible for me to give the dog I am training my undivided attention.

If I am in the house, the puppy is in the house. In the evenings while we are watching television or reading, I allow the puppy to play in the house with the other dogs, but always under my watchful eye. If I am paying bills or showering and unable to pay attention to the puppy, he goes into his crate or kennel. I never, not even for a second, put him in a situation where he can get himself into trouble or develop bad habits.

This practice, in addition to helping ensure the puppy bonds with me, accomplishes two goals. First, any puppy left unsupervised not only develops bad habits but is trouble looking for someplace to happen. It takes all of ninety seconds for an enterprising puppy to turn into a one-puppy demolition team. In record time he can burrow through walls, convert luxurious pillows into

 =

TROUBLE

A word of caution: Problems arise when you attempt to bond with more than one puppy at a time. Say, for example, you decide to keep two puppies from the magnificent litter you bred, or someone makes you an offer you cannot refuse on two puppies. If you go down this road you will need forty-eight hours in each day, because each puppy must be treated as if he were the only one. You must do everything twice. You will need to take each puppy on separate walks, separate rides in the car, separate play sessions, and separate training sessions. You will need to love them, talk to them, snuggle with them, groom them, and play with them separately. They will need to be housed in separate kennels or exercise pens until they have bonded completely with you. Sorry folks, the puppies do not get to entertain and keep each other company while you pay bills, cook dinners, do laundry, mow the lawn or run the kids to and from soccer games. Bonding and socializing is a full-time job with one puppy. Two puppies are downright exhausting. It is not a practice I recommend unless you can commit one hundred percent to both puppies. It has been my experience that one of the puppies will not reach his full potential and eventually one will end up finding a new place to call home. Be smart. Stick with one puppy at a time.

Resist the temptation to take home two puppies!

confetti, gnaw the legs of your glorious Steinway, and as a parting shot leave you an inappropriate and smelly gift on your Oriental rug. Does the expression "I just turned my back for a second!" ring any bells?

Second, there should be some time during each day when a puppy is by himself in his crate or kennel. The time he spends by himself helps him to develop independence and teaches him not to become overly dependent on you. Dogs are social creatures and it is not natural for them to be separated from

their pack for long periods of time. Therefore, it is necessary at an early age to teach puppies to cope with periods of solitude. Puppies that are never left alone can quickly turn into spoiled brats that mistakenly think the world revolves around them. Additionally, they can develop separation anxiety problems. For the competitive canine, separation anxiety problems spell disaster. It will come back to haunt you on the out-of-sight sit-stays or anytime your puppy has to be left alone in a car, motor home, crate, or exercise pen at a show.

As a handler, you can exacerbate the "spoiled brat" syndrome by continually overreacting to a puppy's constant demands. Envision the owner at a training seminar with his puppy situated nearby in an exercise pen or crate. The puppy objects to being away from his owner so he whines. Immediately, the owner jumps up and begins fussing with the puppy—giving him water, sshing him, giving him chewy toys, and so on. When these solutions do not work—and they never do—the owner eventually goes and sits next to his puppy. This only serves to reinforce a puppy's fussiness. The best solution is to meet his needs and then let him learn on his own to behave.

Puppies love the security of a den, whether fancy crate or cardboard box. Photo by Meredith John.

SIMULTANEOUS TRAINING FOR MORE THAN ONE EVENT

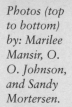

Most trainers of performance dogs want to pursue more than one activity with their dog, so I believe it is necessary to expose a new puppy to all the environments that he will eventually experience. For instance, my Border Collie puppy goes with me when I feed sheep or take the big boys to the field for herding practice. I tie the puppy to the fence to watch while I train. When a pup shows interest in the sheep, I tell him, "See sheep, good boy!" If a puppy slips through the gate and chases a sheep, I let him have fun for a few minutes. Then, when I catch him, I pick him up and carry him away, all the time telling him what a smart boy he is. I never discourage any behavior that I might want to foster at a later date.

Photos (top to bottom) by: Marilee Mansir, O. O. Johnson, and Sandy Mortersen.

I have never made a conscious effort to switch from one activity to another. My dogs and I simply do many things together, starting from the day they move into my house. It becomes a way of life. We live together, go for walks, rides in the car, and to shows and herding events together. Each dog also has his own special training time with me, and does not share that time with anyone else. Because

it is an activity that I personally enjoy, obedience is a very important part of my dogs' lives. But obedience is only a part of their lives.

When I go for walks, I like to take the puppy and let him sniff around the field and trails. I get involved and encourage him to "find." Sometimes I hide behind a tree and get all excited when he finds me. I run around and poke my fingers in holes in the ground and tell him, "Get mousey." I want him to like to look for things so that when we finally do tracking it is just an extension of the games. I personally have never trained an agility dog, but if I did I would have tunnels and little jumps at puppy level so the puppy could learn to jump and climb all over them as a baby. If I had a terrier I would encourage pouncing and digging. I would give him a sandbox and bury treasures for him to find. A Whippet puppy would be encouraged to chase a fuzzy thing whipping around at the end of a pole, and so on.

When teaching obedience behaviors, I simply manipulate the puppy so that his head is up, and I make voice, food, and toys the motivators for that particular body position. Everything is done very consistently so that later, when the puppy is confronted with the obedience routine, it will be his natural response. Dogs learn through consistency, repetition, and association. They easily learn the actions that go with different activities. For example, when we go to the training

Continued on next page.

hall, it is obedience time. But when I pick up my whistle, put on my boots and head for the car, they know we are doing sheep. Conversely, if I pick up the harness, longline and flags, they know we are going to track. To make sure a dog will not be afraid to pull on a tracking line after he has been obedience trained, I let the puppy pull me when I throw things for him. I will toss food or a ball and encourage the puppy to get it while I run behind him, keeping tension on the leash. However, if we are just going for a walk down the street or through a dog show, the same puppy would get a little jerk if the collar tightens. When he looks back I tell him to "Walk nice," and I might play a game of tug with the leash.

Some trainers worry about starting a herding or agility dog in obedience before he learns to herd or run an agility course. They fear that the dog will learn to focus intently on them, and that it will be difficult later to get the dog to focus on stock and work independently. I have never experienced this problem. My puppies learn that I am the provider of *all* the fun things in their lives; therefore they *want* to be *with* me. (This is what I mean when I speak of teaching the dog to *focus* on me—it should not be confused with staring at my face all day or with doing attention heeling. I simply mean teaching him to want to be with me.)

Since dog training began, trainers have taught more than one activity at a time. Winifred Strickland did tracking with all of her obedience Shepherds. Many OTCH Goldens and Labs have Senior Hunter and Master Hunter titles. Jo Johnson's fabulous Sheltie, Hobi, has agility titles that he earned while also showing in obedience every weekend, all over the country, earning seven Ken-L-Ration Dog of the Year awards. A number of breed clubs now offer the Versatility Award. In order to earn this award a dog has to compete in and earn titles or points in at least three different areas. To accomplish this within their relatively short lifetime, dogs must be trained for some events simultaneously. They are incredibly versatile and actually thrive on multiple activities. It gives their lives special meaning and develops a most wonderful relationship with their human partners.

Photos, (top to bottom) by: Tracy Libby, Marilee Mansir, and Meredith John.

I believe our dogs' lives should be wellrounded, just as our own lives should be well balanced in a variety of areas. I spend twenty-four hours with my dogs every day, but only a few hours in the show or trial ring. I want all my dogs to participate enthusiastically in a variety of activities. I have consistently accomplished this goal by using the methods that I share in this book.

Block Two:
Make Training Fun

IF YOU WANT TO BE A GOOD TRAINER YOU need to do three things: Train, train, train. There's no way around it. There are no short cuts. A substantial part of learning to be a proficient trainer is learning how to play with your puppy and how to incorporate play into your training regimen so your puppy views training as fun. I can already hear owners wailing, "For heaven sakes, I know how to play with my puppy!" If that's the case then you have my permission to skip this chapter. However, if you want to know how to use play to create a happy, motivated dog that is focused, attentive, and eager to work in any competitive arena, then read on.

There really is no limit to the fun you can have with your puppy and the behaviors you can instill when you teach your puppy to learn using play. Play creates fun; fun creates focus; and focus maximizes a puppy's propensity to learn. The more your puppy focuses on you, the more you will be able to teach him. The more you play with your puppy, the more he will want to be with you. You will become the most exciting aspect of his world. Subsequently, your puppy will be more attentive to learning and less inclined to wander off and find his own fun or

Play creates fun; fun creates focus; focus maximizes learning.

Puppies spend countless hours playing.

High-play-drive dogs play and cool off after a training session.

PUPPIES POSSESSED

Puppies spend countless hours playing with their littermates: running, freezing, stalking, pouncing, and crouching in preparation for mock battle. Suddenly, they tear off in opposite directions, twisting and turning and running in all-out sprints as they body-slam and somersault and playfully nip each other's ears and necks. At first the play is friendly and good-hearted. As the puppies grow, the ground rules quickly change and the play becomes more fierce and competitive. The puppies are not only establishing a pecking order within their litter, they are also honing their natural prey instincts. These include playing, retrieving, herding, and hunting. As a trainer, you can capitalize on these natural instincts and drives to instill the specific behaviors that produce an enthusiastic and motivated worker.

Like humans, puppies are individuals. Some puppies are born gregarious, happy-go-lucky and ready for any activity at the drop of a hat. The sight of a Frisbee®, ball or tug toy is enough to whip them into a frenzy. Naturally, it takes little incentive to get them to play. Other puppies, particularly toy and non-sporting breeds, do not have a strong play drive. Nevertheless, do not abandon using play to teach specific behaviors to these dogs. It will take more work on your part to activate the prey drive in breeds or individual puppies that lack a strong play drive. (See page 74 for tips on increasing low play/prey drive.)

There are, of course, exceptions to every rule, and the genetic lottery can produce toy breeds with strong play drives and herding and hunting breeds with little or no play drive. However, every puppy has something in his life that he really loves—maybe it's a furry toy for a Beagle, a squeaky toy for a terrier, a raccoon-scented cloth for a Coonhound, or chase recall games for Siberi-

trouble. Equally important, interactive play develops the most compelling aspect of competitive obedience—attention.

Furthermore, play is essential when it comes to establishing a strong bond and a trusting relationship between you and your puppy. A puppy that trusts you will be more open to learning because he has no fear or anxiety, two things which inhibit learning.

Fun and games are vital for stimulating circulation and building strong bones and muscles and a strong heart. Play nourishes and energizes a puppy's mind and keeps it active, healthy, and alert. As puppies grow and mature, play is the perfect prescription for releasing stress during training sessions and while on the campaign trail.

ans and Whippets. In the breed ring, finding that "something" that turns a dog on is often referred to as "pushing a dog's buttons." Basically, it's anything—a toy, a ball, a specific noise or tone of voice—to which a puppy will respond. If you have a puppy with low play drive, then you need to find that "something" that excites and stimulates and drives your puppy to the brink of madness. Then use it *only* to incite play.

If I had a dollar for every time someone told me, "My puppy won't play!" I'd be a wealthy woman living the life of luxury on the French Riviera. There are owners walking among us who are absolutely one-hundred percent convinced that their puppy will not play. Here is the typical scenario. An owner brings their puppy to class and spends the better part of the time moaning about how their puppy won't play. I take the puppy, tweak him and say in a high, squeaky voice, "I've got you! You silly boy," or "Look at you!" Quickly, but gently, I will grab at his feet or tap his feet with my foot or bounce a tug toy. Within ten seconds the puppy is playing with me—a total stranger.

RULES OF ENGAGEMENT

One of the most useful and valuable by-products of play is that your puppy will grow into a spirited, well-adjusted dog that is confident, wild with excitement about training, and anxious to be with you.

The criteria for play are simple. First, you can *play any game your puppy likes, as long as the play is interactive and fun.* (Sitting at your kitchen table drinking coffee or chatting on the telephone while your puppy chases squirrels in the backyard is not interactive play.) Second, you must *teach your puppy to play so that you are the primary object of his interest and fun.* I can't stress enough the im-

Some puppies are born gregarious, happy-go-lucky, ready for any activity at the drop of a hat.

portance of this concept. You must be the most exciting aspect of his world.

If your puppy is bored, who do you think is boring him? If your puppy would rather run off and play with other dogs than play with you, then you are not the most exciting aspect of his world. If you want to succeed in any competitive forum you need to do whatever it takes to make yourself the center of his universe. Your puppy must want and need to be with you more than anything or anyone else in the world. Then you know you are the point of origin for your puppy's fun—the center of his universe.

Third, rather than aimlessly playing or throwing a ball for your puppy, *channel the play into learning specific commands or desired behaviors* in a fun, stress-free environment. This ideology has been championed by Sylvia

> Teach your puppy to play so that you are the primary object of his interest and fun.

Hide and seek or "find me!" is a great game to play to begin teaching the come command. When you are playing with your puppy and he looks away, duck behind a bush or building. Call his name enthusiastically. When he finds you, reward him with a tidbit of food or his favorite toy and plenty of praise. Photo © Lana Young Photography.

Bishop for some thirty years. For example, hide a tasty tidbit of food behind a door or under a bucket and teach your puppy to "Find it." This helps your puppy learn to use his nose and begins building a strong tracking and retrieve drive. Throw a toy and teach your puppy to "Look" before sending him for it. Run down the hall and hide behind a door or chair and call your puppy enthusiastically, "Puppy, Puppy, Puppy." When he finds you, get on the floor and play with him. Make a big fuss and tell him he is a brilliant boy! This begins teaching the "come" command in a fun and exciting manner. If you are playing with your twelve-week-old puppy and he does a "down" on his own—tell him "Good down! Aren't you a clever boy!" If he takes two steps backwards on his own, tell him "Good walk-back!" If he lies flat on his side, tell him "Good flat!" If he kisses your nose, tell him "Good kiss!" If he jumps in the air, tell him "Good jump!" If he rolls over, tell him "Good rollover!"

Put a command to every behavior you want to reinforce. If you are playing and the puppy stops to sniff the ground, take off running in the opposite direction, clap your hands and say his name in an excited tone of voice. Nine out of ten times the puppy will chase you. Tap the ground while you say his name enthusiastically. When he gets close to you, tell him "Good come!" Or try throwing a toy between your legs and encourage him to run through your legs to retrieve it. Next time as he runs through your legs to retrieve the toy, quickly turn around and

"Find it! Good sniff!" Photo by Nan Cochrane.

"Look!" Put a command to every behavior you want to reinforce.

Reinforce the down with "Good down!"

Use play to begin teaching the "over" command by encouraging your puppy to jump over your legs.

Use play to begin teaching the "go through" command by encouraging your puppy to go through your legs.

face him. As he picks up the toy, gently pop the lead towards you and tell him "Good one!" Begin instilling the "over" and "go through" commands utilizing play.

If your goal is obedience titles, throwing a toy between your legs begins teaching the puppy where "front" is and how to come in straight on a recall. When you turn and face the puppy and call him to front, it begins instilling fronts in a fun and exciting manner. Remember, time is of the essence when working with puppies. They grow up quickly. So, rather than playing aimlessly with your puppy, use this time wisely. Use your imagination to develop other fun and exciting games that will instill the behaviors you want to encourage.

Finally, never leave toys lying haphazardly around the training building, dog yard, or house. A chew toy or a basketball in the dog yard is fine, but the only time that the puppy gets to play with the really fun toys should be when he plays with you. You make the toys appear and disappear. Because you control the really fun toys, your puppy will associate playing fun and exciting games with you. You become the primary object of his fun—the center of his universe. Remember, if a puppy is allowed to wander off and play with his favorite toys any time he chooses, he does not need you.

KEEP THE GAMES FUN

Put some energy and creativity into being a fun person. Remember, you always play and train for attitude.

Create Excitement

If you want your puppy to be fun and excited, *you* must be fun and exciting. Be silly and uninhibited. Run through the house or across the yard, moving quickly and clapping your hands. Jump up and down, or hide behind a tree and call your puppy enthusiastically. Lie on the ground and play with him. Scratch his tummy, kiss his nose, bang his toy on the ground or let it bounce off a wall. Occasionally lie flat on the ground and let him crawl up your tummy and smother your face with kisses. If you are slow and methodical, your puppy will grow into a dog that is slow and methodical. If you treat him like a zombie, he'll act like a zombie. If you want to speed up your puppy, speed yourself up. The faster you are, the faster your puppy will be.

Let the Puppy Win

In order to keep your puppy enthusiastic about playing and learning, it is important to let him win equally when you are playing. No one, not even a puppy, likes to play with a bossy, pushy person who constantly monopolizes the toys and the games. When you throw a ball or toy, run with your puppy and pretend you are trying to get it first. When he gets it, clap your hands and tell him, "Look at you! Aren't you

Use your imagination to generate fun. Here Bobbie has thrown a dumbbell through her legs.

clever!" Let him strut around with the toy in his mouth and relish his mammoth achievement. This helps to build his confidence and trust.

Continually taking the toy away from the puppy will cause several problems. First, it will cause him to shut down and subsequently he will learn to find his fun elsewhere. Or he will learn the annoying habit of not retrieving the toy. You will then be stuck playing the "Catch-me-if-you-can" game. Furthermore, if you continually take it away, he will never learn to hold on to the toy. This will come back to haunt you big-time on any retrieve exercise because your puppy inadvertently learned to drop the retrieved item two feet in front of you. Most breeds are susceptible to this type of behavior, so it's imperative that you teach them from the get-go to bring the retrieved item all the way back.

> Channel the play so the puppy learns desired behaviors and commands.

Clap your hands to encourage the puppy to come closer.

Use the toy to bring the puppy into your lap and close to your face. Photos by Lana Young Photography.

Remember Whose Toy It Is

Finally, puppies learn not to play with toys because their owners will not let them play! Six months down the road the owners are complaining, "He doesn't like to play!" or "I can never get him to play." It's not just your toy, it is his toy as well. Let him play with it too. Remember that! As he struts around savoring his victory, tell him he is a clever lad, but keep your hands off the toy for ten or fifteen seconds. If he drops the toy, kick it across the room and run after it, or snatch it up and turn your back on the puppy. Tell him, "It's mine! I've got it." You could drag the toy on the floor and let the puppy chase and catch it. If you don't mind your puppy jumping on you, induce him to bring the toy all the way back by clapping your hands, then tap your chest and encourage him to jump up on you. Ask the puppy to release the toy at chest level. This brings him close to your face where you can indulge him with a cornucopia of hugs and kisses, and then stare adoringly into his eyes and tell him he is a wonderful, clever, brilliant boy! If you have a small breed puppy, kneel on the floor and encourage him to get close to your face. This practice prevents a puppy from developing the annoying habit of dropping the toy midway in anticipation of further play.

Hold the puppy by his buckle collar as you throw the ball again. Give him a little tap on the chest and growl at him, Rrrrrrrr! Ask him, "Do you want to get it?" Say it with excitement! Who cares if the neighbors hear you? Let go of his collar and run with him again, but this time you get the toy. Tell him, "I've got it. It's mine." Drag the toy on the floor in and out and around your legs as he tries to get it. This creates excitement and helps build strong retrieve and play drives. Hold the puppy by the collar again and throw the toy. Before letting go of his collar, gently push him backward and then both of you run for the toy. Pushing backward causes the puppy to drive forward after the toy and really gets his excitement high. This time you both get the toy. Have a tug game or do a "twist" or a "spin" before ending the play session. Remember, when you are playing don't forget to share the toy. A good rule of thumb is that you get the toy, he gets the toy, you both get the toy.

Quit Before the Puppy Tires

A word of caution—don't go overboard with play. Puppies have short attention spans and limited restraint. Your goal is to quit while the puppy craves more. This will ensure that your puppy will be wild about playing the next time you bring out the toys. If you play until the puppy is exhausted or bored and decides it is time to quit, you have played too long and lost control of the game.

PITFALLS TO AVOID

Handlers that fail to achieve excellent results from using interactive play in their training usually do so for one or more of the following reasons.

You Get What You Give

Interactive play requires a healthy dose of energy combined with a dash of enterprising madness. A puppy that has a low play drive can easily double your required energy output. It can be downright exhausting. However, I firmly believe that you get out of a puppy exactly what you put into him. I'll say it again: If you want an adult dog that is one-hundred percent focused on you—a dog that is zippy, animated, enthusiastic, and willing and eager to work both in and out of the ring—then you must put the requisite time, energy, and gusto into instilling those behaviors during his formative years. If you are not willing to work to make yourself the most exciting aspect of your puppy's world, then you are not likely to be successful in competition.

Avoid Negativity

Often, handlers run afoul with their own attitude. The puppy whose owner has a poor attitude will never reach his full potential. Too many trainers have a tendency to be negative. "My puppy doesn't like to play," or "My puppy won't play," they complain. I've heard

Your goal is to quit while your puppy is still craving more. This four-month-old Border Collie is cooling off after a training session.

it a hundred times. Get the idea that your puppy cannot or will not play out of your mind forever!

We are bombarded with negativity everywhere—television, newspapers, radio, and even ringside at dog shows. Negativity is extremely contagious, so it is easy to see why many people slide into the vast chasm of pessimism. However, in order for the human/canine relationship to flourish in a competitive environment, it requires confidence. If you are convinced your puppy cannot or will not play (or retrieve or herd or jump), he will pick up on that negativity and will not feel comfortable playing with you.

So, starting right this minute, you need to empty your mind of any theories, thoughts, notions or preconceived ideas that your puppy cannot or will not play. Believe in your puppy. Truly believe in your heart that your puppy is confident and capable of mastering any task, given the appropriate training and stimulation. Reassure your puppy. Your eyes, voice, facial expression, and mannerism must convey that you are confident that he will succeed.

Eliminate negative words that sabotage you and your dog and replace them with the power of positive speech:

ELIMINATE:	SUBSTITUTE:
self-doubt	self-respect
self-conscious	self-confidence
I have to	I've decided to
anxiety	adrenaline
frustration	enthusiasm
despair	hope
discouraged	exhilarated
depressed	excited

Incite the chase instinct by dragging a toy on the ground. Photo by Lana Young Photography.

Incite the Chase Instinct

Many handlers stand in one spot and try to shove a toy in their puppy's face. When the puppy refuses to grab it, they say in frustration, "He won't play." If you were a puppy, would you play this way? If your puppy will play with other dogs, then he will play with you if you make yourself active, fun and exciting.

Puppies and adult dogs like action. The chase and flight instincts are the strongest instincts they possess. You can teach a puppy to play by inciting the chase instinct. For example, attach his favorite toy to a lunging whip (available at most saddlery shops) or tie a string on the toy and drag it around the room or yard. Drag it in and around your legs and between your feet to build excitement. Remember to always, always, always, move away from your puppy. The goal is to incite the chase instinct. It is virtually impossible to incite a chase instinct if you are moving toward your puppy. Use his natural instincts to your advantage. Some breeds will require a little more effort on your part, but perseverance is the key to success. Do not give up too easily.

Use Toys Discretely

Another area where handlers inadvertently run afoul is by saturating their puppy with dozens and dozens of toys. If a puppy has access to a bucket full of toys all day long, the novelty and excitement will wear off fast. Guaranteed. One day the owner will decide to pick up a toy, and, when the puppy displays the enthusiasm of a rock, the befuddled owner cannot figure out what has gone wrong. Toys are much more appealing and exciting to puppies when they appear only at special times. For instance, you are sitting on the ground talking to your puppy. Suddenly, out of nowhere, you produce his favorite ball or tug toy and the two of you interact with it for a few exciting minutes. You tug it, toss it across the yard, chase it, pounce on it, drag it, shake it, and growl at it. When the game is over the toy disappears until the next training or play session.

Make Play Your Passion

Last but not least, some handlers have a tendency to be lazy when it comes to training their puppies. They want their puppies to accomplish fabulous feats, yet they do not want to exert themselves. Anyone can stand in one spot and throw a ball across the yard while the puppy happily runs back and forth doing all the work. This helps to temporarily tire a puppy, but it does not maximize the human/canine relationship or develop the puppy's personality. Or the handler engages in a game of tug-of-war, but instead of focusing on the puppy, she is thinking "Geez, I forgot to stop and pick up a gallon of milk." Six or eight months later this person wonders why her puppy finds other dogs and people more exciting.

No one said motivating and training a dog for competition is effortless. The energy and passion you put into your puppy during his formative weeks will be repaid tenfold as he grows and begins to endure the rigors of training and competing. I guarantee it.

CONTROLLING THE GAMES

Whether your puppy is chasing a ball or playing a game of tug, it is essential that you teach him some control during the games. Think of how he should behave as an adult dog. It is one thing to be able to whip a dog into a frenzy simply by producing a ball or a tug toy. Allowing him to be totally out of control, however, is a completely different matter. If you want to control your puppy when he is an adult, you must be able to control the play when he is a puppy. Some handlers staunchly profess, "I can't use food or toys because my puppy is obsessed with them. When I take away the food or the toy, he shuts down." This, in my opinion, is a control issue. Guess who is controlling the game?

Praise is a reward for a job well done. Learning to correctly praise is a key component in good training. It is important that you discover the words, sounds or gestures that build a puppy's ego and boost his confidence. Praise is one element that keeps him enthusiastic and eager to continue learning.

Here are some tips to help you praise more effectively:

- If you want a puppy to think about what he is doing but still be happy—the praise should be soothing and quiet but very rewarding. If, for example, he's learning a sit-stay the praise should be calming yet satisfying to the dog. "Good boy" or "That's very nice." The praise should not initiate any action. The puppy receives verbal praise for doing his sit and gets a clear picture of what you want. He learns to hold the position until he is released. Exuberant praise would cause him to break.

- If you want to rev up the puppy, the praise should instigate the behavior. If, for example, the puppy flies back to you on a retrieve or recall, the praise should be, "Super job! That was brilliant!" The intonations in your voice should fluctuate. The puppy should be charged and ready to try again.

- If an exercise has been particularly difficult for a puppy, the praise should be explosive. You are rewarding his effort and courage. The praise will pump up his ego and build his confidence.

- Talking to a puppy incessantly is not praise. "Be careful running around, sweetie. Don't hurt yourself. Be nice to the other dogs. Watch what you're doing. Look out for the stick." It's babble, and ninety percent of the time it is monotone. The lack of oral fluctuation teaches a puppy to ignore you. Save the talking for when the pup has done something worth praising.

- Force yourself to pay attention to what you are saying. Recognize how and when you praise your puppy. Think about what message you are sending.

If you have little or no control over a puppy when you're playing, what will happen in a very exciting situation when he is an adult dog? If a puppy is allowed to cultivate brazen behaviors, such as aggressively snapping at a ball in your hand or knocking you head-over-tea kettle as he lunges for a toy, what will he be like as a one-hundred-pound dog who wants to zig when you want to zag? What will happen if he decides he wants the tug toy you are holding or the tasty hot dog you are eating? If you cannot get a puppy to drop or release a tennis ball, how will you prevent him from swallowing the chicken bone he has gleefully snapped up? If you can't call him back to you when he's chasing a ball, how will you control him in a field full of sheep?

Most control problems start early in the human/canine relationship. Your four-month-old puppy is pushy and grabby when you bring out a toy. You mistakenly think of it as cute puppy behavior so a remedy is never implemented. If you allow this type of behavior to continue, you inadvertently set the course for a myriad of problems later. Soon the puppy is eight months old and nearly taking off your hand as he lunges for the toy.

The remedy is a simple self-correction. If you merely stand on the puppy's leash before bringing out the toy, the puppy will correct himself when he lunges. When he stops lunging and shows some restraint, praise him and then give him the toy. If you do this correctly, after a few times the puppy will realize that lunging and grabbing at the toy is not productive.

Unfortunately, if you fail to recognize and immediately take control when rude and disrespectful behaviors first begin, you inadvertently relinquish your leadership in the human/canine relationship. The puppy has his foot in the proverbial door and is well on his way to being in full control of the situation. He can now dictate how and when things will be done. The situation, if not remedied immediately, will only go from bad to worse. The bottom line is respect. You must teach your puppy, in a fun manner, to respect you. If the puppy does not respect you during play, how can you expect him to respect you in a training or show situation?

Controlling the games allows you to control your puppy. Controlling him as a puppy will allow you to control him as an adult. Control, however, is not

If you want to control your puppy when he is an adult, you must be able to control the play when he is a puppy.

about suppressing a puppy's character or stifling his personality. The right amount of control establishes early on, albeit in a fun and exciting manner, who is boss in the human/canine relationship. Little or no control during puppyhood produces an adult dog that is an incorrigible hoodlum destined to make your life and show career miserable. Too much control, on the other hand, creates an adult dog that is too regimented, stressed, and unsure of himself. This dog, too, will be unable to perform to the best of his abilities. Once you've mastered the right amount of control and established the ground rules, there are no limits to the clever, exciting games you can create. Your play-training time will then produce a competition dog that is eager and willing to perform any task you ask of him.

Block Three: The Finer Points of Motivation

HAVE YOU EVER KNOWN A DOG TO RUN out in the backyard and do obedience exercises by himself because he enjoyed doing them? No. Puppies and adult dogs perform specific commands and exercises because they are motivated to do so. A few dogs will work enthusiastically because they naturally have a great desire to please, but the majority of dogs perform obedience, herding or any other canine activity because their handler makes it fun for them. Puppies are very social creatures. They thrive on attention, and the training and inter-action with their owner gives them the attention they crave.

My Sheltie, Cajun, does not have a great desire to please, but he happily works for me. Cajun successfully completed his Utility Dog title because I worked hard at making obedience fun and exciting for him, and he gets cookies as a reward. On the other hand, my Border Collies do not care about cookies. They love to interact with me on any level—training, showing, herding, fetching a ball, riding in the car, or being groomed.

You must always be your puppy's primary motivation to work, train, and play.

PRIMARY AND SECONDARY MOTIVATORS

Few aspects of training cause handlers more angst than does motivation. To simplify the process, think of motivation in two categories—primary and secondary motivation. If your puppy is to succeed in any competitive environment, his primary motivation must always be you. Early in his life he must learn to work for you—for verbal and physical praise, for play, for fun, and for the love of working. Remember, in most competitive arenas the only motivator you can take into the ring is your relationship with your dog. Therefore, your dog must enjoy being with you.

Secondary motivators include any type of food treat such as liver, chicken, cheese or a tasty tidbit of food. They can also be any type of toy—a tennis ball, soccer ball, stuffed animal, squeaky toy, Frisbee®, stick, tug toy, or ball on a rope. A secondary motivator is basically anything that helps to stimulate and excite your puppy. It is important to note that the toys and food are merely extensions of yourself—that little extra perk that puts some "oomph" into training. You can have all the food and toys in the world, but *you* must always be your puppy's primary source of motivation. There are no substitutes. If your puppy is not tuned in to you—excited and happy about being with you—the toys and the food will not work

As I mentioned in the first chapter, the key to good training is learning to observe your puppy. Find out what he responds to, what type of noise turns him on, what toys or games excite him—in other words, what makes him tick. Once you identify these characteristics it is much easier to develop a training program tailored to the individual dog.

Secondary motivators can be anything that excites and stimulates your puppy. Photo by Dannie Whall.

The key to good training is finding out what makes your puppy tick.

Both primary and secondary motivators are used to teach a five-month-old Afghan the tunnel. Photo courtesy Diane Bauman.

THE HANDLER'S VOICE

The handler's voice is his or her greatest primary motivator and training tool. If I talk to my dogs in a normal tone of voice, they become happy, attentive, and wag their tails. If I make my voice high-pitched and excited, they become excited. If I change my tone just the tiniest bit and say "ah ah" or "no," their ears go back, their heads drop, and their tails go down. If I am talking to a puppy and the other dogs hear me, they fly across the yard to find out what we are doing. My voice is the one motivator that I can take with me in any place or situation. Unfortunately, the voice is the training tool that is least effectively utilized by handlers.

> **Pay attention to the sound of your voice. It's the best motivator you have!**

If you want to maintain your dog's attention when in competition, you must build that response in him while he is young. Learn how to pique your puppy's interest and attention by talking to him in a play situation. *It is one of the most important lessons he will learn.*

The best way to motivate your puppy is to motivate yourself. If you want a puppy that is excited about working, then you must be motivating and exciting. The next time you train, play, or talk to your puppy, pay particular attention to the sound of your voice. When the puppy comes charging toward you, does your voice reflect excitement? When your puppy retrieves a stick or ball, does your voice say, "Excellent! Look at you!"? When your puppy takes two steps in heel position or successfully maneuvers the dog walk, does your voice encourage and motivate him? Are his ears and tail up? Is he pleased with himself? Or is he frightened and cowering because your voice is abrupt, loud, and filled with negativity? Is he bored to death because you drone on and on in the same monotonous tone regardless of his achievements? I have seen well-intentioned handlers go through an entire training session and never change the tone of their voice. "Good dog. Heel. Heel. Heel. No. Stop that. Good dog." The words run together and the only message the puppy gets is, "Here we go again—that same old boring voice droning on and on and on." If you were a puppy, would you be motivated?

This eleven-week-old puppy is both inquisitive and attentive to his handler's voice.

If you want to be successful in a competitive environment, you must continue to motivate your dog throughout his show career.

Puppies are easily distracted by peripheral stimuli like birds, trees, lawn furniture, shadows, leaves blowing in the wind, clouds rolling by, dust settling, other dogs and people, strange noises, and so forth. If you want a dog's undivided attention, you must teach him to pay attention during his formative months. Give him a reason to focus on you. Remember: You must become the most exciting aspect of his world. The more proficient you are at motivating the puppy with your voice, the fewer corrections you will need as he enters the rebellious stages of development.

The rebellious or "juvenile" stage is generally characterized as puberty or adolescence. The age at which a puppy enters this stage varies greatly as puppies mature at different rates. Smaller breeds tend to mature faster than larger breeds. For instance, a ten-month-old Sheltie is generally through the rebellious stage and close to maturity. A ten-month-old Border Collie is a pain in the rear. He's dead center in the middle of adolescence. A Great Pyrenees, on the other hand, is still a baby at eighteen months.

Behaviors associated with adolescence include the dog showing his independence, ignoring you, testing you, or being very distracted and inattentive. It is a trying time for handlers. Many handlers are unprepared for the influx of emotions and behaviors that accompany a puppy in this stage. Anyone who has survived their child's teenage years can relate. It takes more than patience alone to survive your puppy's adolescence. It takes perseverance and a keen recognition and understanding of the accompanying behaviors. However, it is important to recognize this stage and work through it.

When my Border Collie, Rio, was about one year old and going through adolescence, I did not think either one of us would survive it. I had to work extra hard to keep his attention and focus on the task at hand. Every day I would remind myself that it was a stage he was going through; it would pass. It did pass, and Rio matured into a fabulous competition dog.

Even after your dog begins his competitive career, you must continue to be exciting and stimulating. Whether he is twelve weeks or six years old, you must still be the most exciting aspect of his world. If you want to succeed in competitive events, then you should continue to motivate and stimulate your dog throughout his career. Unless a dog continues to receive positive interaction and motivation from his owner, he will eventually shut down. Even though he knows the job, he will lose interest in obeying the repetitive, boring instructions.

PLAY AND GAMES

As mentioned throughout this book, play is an *excellent* motivator—right at the top of the list along with a handler's voice. In addition to being interactive and fun, *play and training should be integrated so that it is difficult, if not impossible, for the puppy to distinguish between the two.* There should never be a demarcation line that conveys to the puppy, "This is playing and this is training." Training should be incorporated into playing, and vice versa so that each training session becomes a fun lesson. It is work for you, the handler. In fact, it can be downright exhausting some days. Exerting your muscles—physical or mental—is tiring. Yet, simultaneously you should feel invigorated and motivated after a training and play session. You should have a sense of accomplishment and satisfaction.

Many handlers mistakenly train, train, train, and then end the session by playing fun games with the puppy. This produces a puppy that cannot focus on the task at hand. His goal will be to hurry and finish training because play-

FOR SUCCESS IN THE CONFORMATION RING

Learning to use all the motivators in this section can help your conformation prospect be more successful too. Here are some specific things you can do:

1. Start teaching the routines of gaiting and being examined when your puppy is eight to twelve weeks of age.

2. Make conformation practice seem like fun and games to the puppy.

3. Inject plenty of play and praise into your training sessions.

4. Remember, your voice is the one motivator you will always have with you. If your dog responds to it, you won't panic when you run out of bait or forget his favorite squeaky toy.

5. Use play training as motivation all through the dog's conformation career. Never let the show routine become boring.

6. If you are the most exciting thing in your dog's world, the judges will take notice of the rapport between you. They are more likely to put up a dog that enjoys showing and responds positively to his handler.

ing is more exciting. A better plan is to play, train, play. Integrate playing into training and vice versa to continually maintain the puppy's interest and enthusiasm. The last thing you want is a puppy that wanders off because he is bored while playing. Remember, if your puppy is bored, guess who is boring him? If you cannot keep your puppy's attention on you during playtime, it will be impossible to maintain his attention in the myriad of distractions present in a competitive situation.

A four-month-old black Lab begins learning the "heel" position. Food is used to lure his head into the correct position. Photo © Lana Young Photography.

Make the transition between playing and training indistinguishable. For example, play, play, play, and then quickly lure the puppy into a sit by gently tucking his rear. Immediately praise him, "Good sit!" or "Look at you!" Then move directly into playing again. Throw a tug toy or ball between your legs, or drag it on the floor and encourage him to chase it. This type of play builds a solid play and retrieve drive. If you play tug-of-war, let the puppy tug, tug, tug, and then release the tension on the toy so he quickly folds into a down. Praise him lavishly with "Good down!" Gently tug, tug, tug again, pulling up on the toy so the puppy moves from a down to a sit. Tell him, "Good sit!" or "Yea for you!" When he is tugging on a toy, pivot your body into heel position and take two or three steps using the toy to lure the puppy into correct heel position and keep him there for two or three seconds. Ask him, "Are you doing your heel work?" Release, play and repeat.

If you are playing with a toy and the puppy drops it, snatch it up and quickly toss it behind him. Encourage him to "Get it!" Try to beat him to the toy. Then, drag it on the floor as you encourage the puppy to chase it. Play and train continually from one exercise to another in order to maximize the motivation and keep the puppy's attention on you at all times.

A young puppy has a very limited attention span, so it is imperative that you keep the excitement going. If you allow a lull or a break in the playing, the puppy will lose interest and more often than not will wander off to find his own fun. The goal is to keep your puppy's attention on you, which means you must be more exciting and stimulating than his surroundings. As he grows and matures, begin asking him for more responsibility, including longer periods of continuous attention.

It will take a great deal of energy, spontaneity, and creative thinking on your part to keep a puppy focused and attentive. If you want your puppy's undivided attention, make sure he has *your* full attention. Do not contemplate what you are going to serve for dinner or fret over the increasing number of weeds in your garden while you are training. Your puppy and the behaviors you are attempting to instill should be the only thing on your mind at that time. If done correctly, ten minutes of play and training will get the puppy wound up. You, on the other hand, may be ready for a two-hour nap! Remember, puppies have limited attention spans. Always quit while your puppy is still excited to ensure that he will want to play again next time.

The transition between playing and training should be indistinguishable.

The handler uses play to teach a puppy the "down" command.

If your puppy wanders off, never stop training. Do something funny or exciting to get his attention back on you. Photo © Robert and Eunice Pearcy.

To generate enthusiasm, lie on the ground as you call your puppy. Encourage him to crawl on your tummy.

Smother him with praise and kisses. Photos © Lana Young Photography.

IF YOUR PUPPY WANDERS . . .

A word of caution: If you are playing with your puppy and he decides to sniff some leaves or chase a paper bag blowing in the wind, do not, under any circumstances, stop training and playing at this point. Never think, "Okay, he's tired. He doesn't want to play any more," and stop working. Do not make excuses for your puppy. If you allowed him to wander off, you must do something to pique his interest and create in him the desire to come running back to you.

As I mentioned earlier, you can try doing silly things like falling on the ground, doing a somersault, hopping on one leg, or making funny noises. You can step on his leash or longline and then tell him "I got you, you silly boy!" When he comes to you *always* praise him. Smother him with kisses and tell him he is adorable. As soon as his attention is back on you, it is important that you do a couple of sits, a down, or a retrieve. You must control the situation.

If you allow the puppy to develop a habit of quitting on his own and wandering off during play, that attitude will rear its ugly head throughout his training and eventually in the ring. He will quit when the going gets tough in a competitive environment because he was allowed to do so in training. He learned that he could establish and follow his own rules regardless of your desires.

Trip, Stumble and Fall

If your six-month-old puppy is interested in everything except you when you take him out to play, you should be concerned. If he shows zero interest when you talk to him but goes nuts and wants to play when you show him his favorite toy, what is his primary motivator? Somewhere along the line you inadvertently let his toy become the primary motivator. Unfortunately, when you put the toy away your puppy will shut down. He will most likely wander off and find his own fun. He thinks that the toys are fun but you are dull. The secondary *motivator* is not the problem; not using it correctly is the problem.

In this case you must go back and re-establish yourself as your puppy's primary source of fun. For instance, if your puppy comes up to you and initiates play, immediately seize the opportunity. As before, try rolling around on the floor with him or lie on your back and gently bounce him on your chest. Kiss his nose and make funny noises to arouse his curiosity. Hide behind a door and call his name. Sit on the ground and encourage him to jump over your legs, then do one or two sits or downs. Your mannerisms, enthusiasm, physical and verbal praise—not the toy—should be his reward. All of these things will help to reinforce the idea that you are your puppy's primary source of fun. After you get your puppy tuned in to you again, then bring out a toy and interact with him.

BONE APPÉTIT

Like play and toys, food is a valuable training aid. You can use food to teach virtually any trick or exercise, from heeling to jumping, from recalls to retrieving. Tasty tidbits of food can be used to lure a puppy into the correct position, to expedite learning, or to create a desired response. As the puppy begins to understand what you want, the food quickly becomes a reward rather than a lure. For instance, if you use a tidbit of food to lure your puppy into a "sit," within a week or two the puppy should grasp the concept of "sit." The food is then used as a reward rather than a lure.

Motivating a puppy with food has fallen out of favor with many handlers. They claim puppies become too dependent on food and therefore turn in poor performances in the ring. The problem is not the food. The problem is using the food incorrectly. Most handlers run afoul because they inadvertently teach their puppy that the food is the primary motivator. This is the kiss of death in dog training. When the food disappears, and it always does when you go in the ring (except for breed), the dog naturally shuts down because his motivation to work is gone. No food, no work. It is not the dog's fault. He is just doing what he has been taught to do—work when food is present and quit working when the food disappears. Somewhere along the line that philosophy has been reinforced in the puppy's mind. That is why it is so important that you are always the puppy's primary motivator.

Using food correctly as a motivator is not difficult if you have a clear and concise picture of what you are attempting to accomplish throughout each stage of training. I will use the "down" command to illustrate how I utilize food as a motivator. First, I kneel or sit on the floor with the puppy (I like to get down to his level so I am not towering over him) and I use a tasty tidbit of food to lure him into the "down" position. (Instead of the traditional method of "down," I teach puppies to "fold" into a down. See page 106.) I continue to lure the puppy into a "down" for the first week or two. The puppy simply follows the food into the correct position. The food is always visible and it is virtually impossible for him to make a mistake. I reward the puppy

When used correctly, food is a valuable training aid. Photo courtesy Diane Bauman.

for each correct response. Soon he puts two and two together and he begins to anticipate the command. Anticipation is good. It confirms that the puppy is beginning to learn. As a result he is taking the initiative and trying to perform the behavior on his own.

Unfortunately, what is great progress for a puppy can quickly turn into dangerous territory for the handler. If a handler is going to make a mistake with food training, this is where the problem arises. It is difficult for handlers to stop using food. Some handlers continue to lure a puppy into position for months on end, when he is actually capable of much more responsibility. At some point a puppy must learn to perform the command on his own, without food. The food then becomes a reward, rather than a lure. If food is always present, it will become the primary motivator. Two years later the handler will wonder why his dog shuts down in the ring.

To avoid this problem, once I have lured the puppy into position for a time

Food is a valuable training aid.

and he begins to take the initiative, I move to the next step. I continue to kneel on the floor so I am close to his level. I hide some food in my mouth or behind my back, invisible to the puppy, and while he is standing I say his name and "Down." If he goes into the down position, I verbally praise him with "Good down!" Immediately, I reward him with a tidbit of food while he is still in the down position. Then I release him, telling him again what a brilliant boy he is. I will repeat this process five or six times in succession several times throughout the day to reinforce the command.

If, when I say "down," he stands there staring at me as if I have a third eye, I simply put my hands in his collar and gently guide him into the down position saying "That's your down." He gets no cookies—not even a crumb—until he responds to the command on his own. Then he gets a jackpot full of cookies.

This is the point at which some handlers want to show the puppy that they mean business by jerking him into the down position. How much fun is that? Your puppy will associate the jerk with the down. Guess what he will soon try to avoid?

Do not give up. Persevere. Learning to work without food as a lure is new territory for your puppy. Rather than correct him, help him to understand exactly what you want. If you never require him to perform the behavior without food, he will stagnate in his training. Food will become his primary motivation and he will not perform without it.

Usually, that is not the end of it. The next day he may not respond to the down command at all. He might react as if he has never heard the word "down" word in his life. Do not panic. Expect the unexpected. Simply repeat the above process of asking him to "down." If your puppy complies, praise him and reward him with a tidbit. If there is noncompliance, place your hands in his buckle collar and put him in the down position. Tell him, "That's your down," and release him. Play with him and try it again. When he responds to the command on his own, give plenty of praise and cookies.

When the puppy is responding reliably to the verbal command (without the food being present), move on to the next step. Now the puppy must learn to perform the command unconditionally on his own. At this point, the food begins to appear randomly. It might appear after the first response, the third response, every other response, and so on. Now the puppy is learning to work for you—for fun and praise—rather than for food alone.

At this stage, if your puppy refuses to comply with the "down" command for whatever reason, the worst mistake you can make is to pull out a cookie and coax him down. Never, under any circumstances, go down that road. It will come back to haunt you big-time. All you are doing is bribing your puppy. You are saying, "Please, oh please, do this and I'll give you some tasty food."

Guess who is controlling the situation? Guess who will be controlling the situation when you go in the ring and don't have any bribes? If you teach your puppy to work for praise and for the love of working, then when you need him to come through for you, he will.

Recently someone asked me, "At what point do you take the food away?" I never completely stop using food as a reward. Eventually it begins to appear randomly, but I never stop using food rewards, even with my older dogs. Food rewards, if used correctly, help to reinforce and continue to build enthusiasm, energy, and drive.

COMBINING MOTIVATORS

When your puppy is first exposed to a variety of different motivators, it is not unusual for him to shut down when one of the motivators suddenly disappears. For example, if you are playing the Cookie Toss game and, suddenly, you throw a toy instead of a tasty morsel of food, your puppy is likely to respond with a look of astonishment. More than likely, he will run around sniffing the ground as if thinking "What the heck . . . where's my cookie?" The toy will probably be of little or no interest to him at this point. It is important that you continue, in a firm and determined (but fun) manner, to encourage the puppy to play with the toy.

Try dragging the toy on the floor or kicking it across the room, encouraging him to pick it up. If that fails, try bouncing the toy off the wall or holding it over your head as you tell the puppy, "It's mine. I've got it." Puppies always want whatever they can't have. Encourage the puppy to play by bouncing the toy on his rear. Puppies love that. Drag it in and around your legs to build some excitement. Don't give up. Plow ahead. Be firm and indefatigable until he shows some interest or excitement about the toy.

Build enthusiasm and excitement by attaching a longline to a toy. Drag the toy on the ground and encourage the puppy to chase it. Photo © Lana Young Photography.

Sometimes when I want to use a toy as a motivator, I will do all of my playing and training first. Then, I will move on to the exercises where I want to use food as a motivator. That should not be interpreted as an excuse to avoid dealing with the problems that arise when working with multiple motivators. If your puppy shuts down when you put away the food and bring out a toy, you need to deal with the situation. Do not avoid it.

The goal is to prevent your puppy from becoming overly dependent on either food or a specific toy. When you play with your puppy, keep several different toys handy. Mix them up, thereby generating additional excitement and enthusiasm. If your puppy is not a complete workaholic, you will need to vary the toys to keep him stimulated. For instance, throw a ball across the room and send your puppy for it. Pick up a squeaky toy and, when your puppy heads back to you

Multiple motivators generate excitement.

with the ball, show him the squeaky toy and say, "Look what I've got!" This will encourage him to hurry back to you. You might have a quick tug game and then throw the squeaky toy across the room and send your puppy for it. Pick up a third toy—perhaps a rubber hose or Frisbee®—and when he heads back to you, show him the item as before. Throw it between your legs as you tell him to "get it."

Later, when you are actively campaigning your dog, you will be able to motivate and stimulate him not only with your voice but with a wide variety of secondary motivators. If you forget his favorite ball or cookie on your way to a trial, you will not have to worry. The time and energy you spent building a strong play drive with multiple secondary motivators will get you through the day.

CAJUN, THE INDEPENDENT DOG

Everyone loves Cajun. He's cute, energetic and beguiling. He commands attention wherever he goes. Beneath his captivating exterior is a Shetland Sheepdog with an independent streak. Shelties can be sensitive or insecure. Some are downright wimpy. Therefore, an independent streak is good as long as it's not too strong. It shows that the puppy has some self-confidence. It also helps to give them the "edge" they need to work in a competitive situation.

I acquired Cajun at eight and a half weeks. His independent streak was evident from the start. He resented compulsion or discipline. He hated to be picked up and held. He would go passive in my arms and turn his head away as if unable to endure the situation. He resented any kind of roughhousing and would pin his ears back and try to get away.

As a puppy, Cajun liked to play but he loved food more. From day one, food was very important to him. The problem was that when I brought out the food, Cajun had no further interest in playing. It would have been easier to discard any attempt at play training and reinforce the food training. However, I like options in my training. Play training is important to me because I like using multiple motivators, so I knew I needed to work on encouraging both food and play. Tugging on a leash and playing are motivators that I can take into any competitive ring.

To overcome this problem, whenever Cajun focused only on food and wanted nothing to do with playing, I would put the food away and kick a ball around. Or, I would encourage him to tug on his leash or chase me. I would drag a tug toy between my legs and encourage him to "get it." I persevered until he showed some interest in playing. When he started playing again, his attitude bounced back.

The worst mistake a handler can make is to buy into the "he doesn't like to do that" ideology. From an early age puppies must learn (in a fun manner) that they don't get to control the situation.

Cajun was an adorable puppy when things were going his way, but he was (and still is) a quitter. Because of his independent streak I tried to maintain a 90/10 balance. I compromised a great deal to keep him thinking that he got to do it his way. Ninety percent of the time I kept his training positive, exciting, and active. This kept his attitude upbeat and eager to continue learning and training. I set him up to always succeed so he would not have to be corrected. I never started a training session without first playing with him. That way he always started with a positive attitude.

As Cajun matured and became solid on his exercises, I taught him that he had to do the exercise regardless of the circumstances. If I sent him for a glove and he got the wrong one, I would take him by the collar and show him the right one. He resented that action. He would pin his ears back and want to quit on the spot. He would go through an annoyed stage. This was the ten percent where Cajun needed to understand that regardless of his attitude, he had to do the exercise. He was not allowed to quit because he didn't like it. Once we worked through the problem, his attitude always bounced back.

I continue this practice in his training today. It has helped Cajun grow into a successful and competitive obedience dog. At five years old he has two UDX legs and three High in Trials.

Bobbie Anderson and Cajun taking High in Trial.

Block Four:
Maximize Praise

NOT ALL PUPPIES ARE CREATED EQUAL. In fact, no two puppies are alike. What constitutes praise for one puppy is completely different for another. If you talk to one puppy in a normal, happy tone of voice, he will be excited and attentive and wag his tail. Another puppy will strut around bursting with pride when he is simply rewarded with, "Good boy!" Other puppies are more responsive to low, soothing tones and will stare at you adoringly as they wait to see what you will do.

Praise is a reward for a job well done. The type of praise and how much praise your puppy needs depends on his personality. As you play, train and forge a solid relationship with your puppy, you become more proficient at reading his body language. You learn when and how to praise effectively in order to feed his ego and boost his confidence. This, in turn, stimulates and encourages him to continue learning.

Just as puppies are different in personality and temperament, so, too, are handlers. Some handlers are gregarious and full of energy. They have no problem acting silly and animated with their puppy. Other handlers are more self-conscious. Some handlers are downright lackadaisical. They do not want to put the effort into verbalizing praise. It is much easier, although not nearly as productive, to give a piece of food as a reward than to use verbal energy to make the puppy feel good when he has done well.

TONE OF VOICE

When praising a puppy, vary the tone of your voice and the amount of praise to fit the circumstance. Use enough praise to let him know he is right, but not so much as to make him wild and crazy or to distract him from the task at hand.

For example, if I am playing with my ten-week-old puppy and he does a "sit," I tell him, "Look at you! What a good sit!", or "Aren't you clever!" Once he begins to respond to the verbal command, simply "Good boy!" or "Good sit," is sufficient. It is overkill when a handler jumps up and down hysterically, clapping his hands and screaming, "What a fantastic puppy!" Praise does not need to be loud to be meaningful. Equally important, praise must be sincere. Puppies are not easily fooled by insincerity.

As the length of time my puppy is able to hold his sit progresses, I might praise him with, "What a good sit!" If he holds his sit while other dogs run and play fifteen feet away, I make the

Praise is a reward for a job well-done. An eleven-week-old puppy receives verbal praise and a cookie for doing his sit.

praise more exciting, such as "That was excellent! You are such a good boy!" (But do not make it so exhilarating as to cause him to break his sit-stay. An overdose of praise at this point will distract him from the exercise he is attempting to learn.)

However, if a puppy has been working on an exercise that is particularly difficult for him, such as retrieving, when he finally accomplishes the task your praise should be a display of fireworks. It is a joy in that situation to see the puppy so pleased with himself. However, if all the praise you give—even for the tiniest accomplishment—is explosive, the meaning will be lost. If you are wild with praise when your puppy comes from two feet away, how much praise will he need when he comes quickly on command with distractions all around him? On the other end of the spectrum, if everything the puppy did brought nothing more than a boring, monotone, "Good dog," why would he try any harder?

I always vary the praise words that I use. Sometimes I tell the puppy he is brilliant, clever, or awesome. Another time I will tell him he is terrific, handsome, cute, silly, or smart. The words themselves are not critical, but the tone of voice is vital. Always make an effort to vary your praise words. Even "Good boy" or "good Dog," if used over and over again, will eventually bore your puppy, regardless of the tone of your voice.

Praise is a reward for a job well done. The type of praise your puppy needs depends on the puppy's personality. Learn what kind of praise and how much praise your individual puppy needs. Then praise at the right time, and praise according to the level of accomplishments.

During verbal praise does your puppy stare adoringly at you? Photo © Toni Tucker.

PHYSICAL PRAISE

Use a lot of physical praise, too. Tap your puppy on his shoulder and tell him he is wonderful. Kiss his nose, or get on the ground and hug him when he learns a particular behavior. However, you must be careful because, depending on the individual, physical praise or even the anticipation of physical praise is too stimulating for some puppies and they are unable to concentrate on the task at hand. Another potential problem is that some puppies have a tendency to look away when they are being petted. In this case, verbal praise is more effective. Speak to the puppy in a soothing tone of voice and he probably will stare adoringly at you.

TIMING

The single most important factor in mastering effective praise is timing. Timing is critical. If your timing is off, your praise is worthless. Praise given three seconds after the fact will not tell the puppy what you liked. Puppies learn through repetition, consistency, and association. Poor timing only confuses them.

Timing is critical when giving praise. This handler is praising her dog for an excellent sit during the Sit-Stay exercise.

Praise the instant the puppy grabs the dumbbell or toy. The correct timing of praise tells the puppy exactly what you want.

Puppies learn through repetition and consistency. An eleven-week-old puppy receives verbal praise and a tidbit of food while in the correct heel position.

This five-month old Golden Retriever is learning a "go-out." He should be praised immediately when his nose touches the baby gate.

I cannot stress enough the importance of accurate timing. Let me use the "sit-stay" or "down-stay" exercise as an example. Typically what happens is that the puppy does a marvelous job on his stay exercise, but he receives absolutely no praise until after the entire exercise is complete. When the puppy finally is released from his stay, the handler goes crazy with praise. He has just taught the puppy that the best part of the exercise is when it is over! Praise should always come *during* the "stay" exercise so that the handler reinforces the desired behavior—the puppy doing his "stay." Never make praise a signal that the exercise is finished.

INCORRECT PRAISE

Endless Chatter

Perhaps Sgt. Joe Friday's famous admonishment, "Just the facts, ma'am," says it best. Your praise should not be chronic chatter that develops a life of its own and goes on and on and on. Endless chatter is an extension of poor timing or, more appropriately, a lack of any timing whatsoever. This is an area where handlers can inadvertently fall short. They assume the endless cheerleading is helping. Instead, when a puppy hears drawn out, conversational chatter, or continuous praise, he cannot determine why he is being praised. He is unable to relate the praise to a single behavior. Consequently, he never gets a sense of any one behavior you like. Furthermore, when handlers praise continuously, they inevitably end up praising the puppy at the very moment he is looking away or is out of position. Remember, *praise is a reward for a job well done*—it should never be a gift for every move the puppy makes.

Constant cheerleading can teach a puppy to become overly dependent on praise. Just like a puppy that becomes excessively dependent on food, the puppy that receives constant praise will

FOR PRAISING EFFECTIVELY

Learn to read your puppy so that you know which type of praise and how much praise he needs.

Vary the tone of your voice and the amount of praise to fit the circumstances.

Praise sincerely.

Vary the praise words that you use to prevent boredom.

Use plenty of physical praise, too.

Timing is the most important factor in praising effectively.

Don't nag or constantly chatter at your puppy.

Use praise only as a reward for good behavior, and not for finishing an exercise.

shut down when the praise stops. He has not learned to work without praise. This is an enormous problem in a competitive environment where a handler must work quietly. When the dog is required to perform without his handler talking, he will think something is wrong and his performance will suffer.

While they are teaching the "recall" or "come" command, some handlers begin praising the moment the puppy starts toward them and continue until he reaches them. Such continuous praise takes all the responsibility off the puppy and inadvertently produces an adult dog with a slow recall. The puppy becomes so dependent on constant praise and chatter that he is not able to perform the exercise without it.

When I am teaching the "come" command, I will usually praise with one "Good boy!" as my puppy starts toward me. That one "Good boy!" is then given at varying spots in the recall, as opposed to the same spot each time. For example, in the beginning I give one "Good boy!" as my puppy starts and turns toward me. The next time I might give the "Good boy!" when he is halfway, a third of the way, or two-thirds of the way to me. The point is, I only give *one* "Good boy," and I vary when during the exercise I give it. Eventually, I will give the praise only when the puppy reaches me.

Let's say you have been diligently working on the recall exercise with your eight- or nine-month-old puppy. One day he suddenly slows down about halfway to you. Perhaps he is anticipating a "down" command, or maybe he is confused or unsure of himself. In this instance, let the puppy work through the situation rather than give him additional commands. If, when he starts to slow down, you give a second "come" command or encourage him with "Good boy! C'mon, you can do it," you have assumed the responsibility for his behavior. Instead, give him an opportunity to think through the exercise. When your puppy works through the problem by himself, he will end up with a more reliable recall.

Indiscriminate Praise

Indiscriminate praise is another area where handlers often get into trouble. For example, after your puppy *understands* the command to sit, you tell him "Sit." He starts to obey but midway he chooses not to sit after all, so you help him by tucking his rear. If you praise him, "Good sit!" and reward him with a cookie, what have you taught him? He will think, "It doesn't matter if I sit because Mom will help me. I don't have to be responsible for my behavior." If you do the work for him and he gets a cookie and praise regardless, why should he try harder?

A sterling example of indiscriminate praise is when a puppy is lagging in the heel position and the handler pats his leg and says to the puppy, "C'mon, good boy." The handler has just praised the dog for lagging. The puppy does not have the mental capacity to decode what you said from what you really meant to say. He hears "Good boy" and thinks he is in the correct position. Six or eight months later he gets jerked with a choke chain for lagging. No wonder the dog gets confused and shuts down. If your junior puppy is lagging in heel position, say nothing, but take off running. Your puppy will have no choice except to catch up with you. When he is in the correct position, praise him. "Good boy! That's your heel work!"

Another example of handler error is when a puppy sniffs some collective aromas on the ground and the handler drags him away from the forbidden smells, simultaneously praising, "Good boy." What is so good about it? You have to think about the message you are sending your puppy.

> **Praise is not chronic chatter nor constant cheerleading.**

Nagging

Remember that I said using food as the primary motivator is the kiss of death in dog training? Well, nagging a puppy (or adult dog) is a close second. If you constantly say your puppy's name and nothing happens, you are nagging him and teaching him to be indifferent to your voice. For example, your four-month-old puppy is sniffing a pile of leaves and you say his name, "Fido." He ignores you, so you repeat, "Fido." Again he ignores you. Maybe you repeat his name louder the third time because, obviously, he did not hear you the first two times. Then, after the third time you decide to ignore the entire situation because you do not want to bother going over to your puppy and getting his attention. What have you taught him? In addition to being indifferent to your voice, he has just learned that it is okay for him to make his own decisions and do as he pleases because you will not do anything about his inattention. Always try to look at your actions and the timing of your praise from the puppy's perspective. What message are you sending to him?

LEARNING TO SIT AND ACCEPT PRAISE

It is highly important for every young puppy to learn to sit calmly and attentively while the handler verbally and physically praises him. The praise should be calm and reassuring such as, "Good boy," or "Good job." If the praise is too loud and energetic it will cause the puppy to break. This defeats the purse of the exercise. Every puppy should be taught to sit and accept calm, physical contact such as checking his ears, eyes, or teeth, or counting his toes. The puppy should also accept these behaviors along with calm verbal praise.

Remember, praise is always a reward for good behavior. Verbal or physical praise should never signal that an exercise is finished.

Never drag your puppy to you when he stops to sniff and simultaneously praise him—for example, "Come on, that's a good boy!" Think about the message you are sending to your puppy.

When teaching "Come," praise your puppy the instant he starts to move toward you. Photo © Robert and Eunice Pearcy.

PUPPY TRAINING TIPS FOR AGILITY

- Begin interacting with your puppy as early as five or six weeks, if possible. Otherwise, start as soon as he arrives at your home.

- Expose the puppy to fun games and concepts that he will eventually learn to associate with agility. Teach him to follow food in your hand, circle left, circle right, climb over obstacles, and so on.

- Instill a positive association with the agility equipment by allowing him to explore it in a safe environment. For example, allow him to wander around the equipment, play near the entrance to the chute, or find tidbits of food in the tunnel or on the dogwalk.

- Keep all equipment low to the ground. Your puppy's safety should be paramount. Save jumping until the puppy is over six months of age.

Top photo courtesy Diane Bauman.

- Encourage speed at a young age. If your puppy wants to gallop across a low dogwalk, let him.

- Prepare the puppy for the show environment. Early on, teach him that traveling, riding in a crate, crowds, applause, cheering and so forth make life exciting and fun.

Block Five:
Compulsion and Correction

CORRECTIONS SHOULD NOT BE THE staple of your puppy's training. If you do your job properly and lay the groundwork for a successful working relationship with your puppy, you should have little need for corrections as your puppy grows and matures. The key to raising a well-behaved puppy is management. You manage the puppy and his environment so he develops good habits. Unfortunately many exceptionally talented puppies have been turned off to working because of human error, ignorance or insensitivity. It is an unhappy fact that overcorrection or improper correction can cause puppies to conclude that training and competing are not fun.

There is no such thing as a perfect world where puppies, or adult dogs, never get into trouble. That would be paradise! We all suffer the consequences of our actions, either through rewards or some form of punishment. It is not unfair to say to a puppy, "No, you cannot do that," provided you have done your part and given him plenty of opportunity to learn.

It is your job as a responsible trainer to make training fun and enjoyable for your puppy. A handler directs a future tracking dog's attention toward the track. Photo by Stephen Cochrane.

A puppy learns the acquired behavior of coming quickly and enthusiastically. To encourage the behavior, the handler sits on the ground and enthusiastically calls the puppy's name, while showing him a toy. The reward for coming is the toy.

comply nor repeat commands while the puppy defies them.

It is difficult, if not impossible, to define in black and white all of the circumstances surrounding if and when a correction is warranted and how much correction is reasonable. There are many internal and external influences that can cause a puppy to bungle a command. It is irresponsible to say that if a puppy ignores a "sit" command he deserves a correction, or to tell you that if he refuses to come when called, you should give a correction. You must be very careful not to correct a puppy that is doing what he thinks you want (even though it happens to be the wrong thing) because you gave him the wrong message.

One constant in dog training is that things are not always as they appear. Acquiring the ability to read a puppy's body language and knowing when he is confused, frightened, worried, trying to comply, or blatantly disobeying a command is what separates the good handlers from the great handlers.

TRAINING *IS* COMPULSION

Over the years I have heard well-intentioned trainers exclaim, "I never use compulsion in my training." I honestly do not know how to train without compulsion. All training is compulsion training. Webster defines compulsion as "the act of compelling or state of being compelled." Using that definition, it's easy to see why all dog training—from house training to retrieving—is a form of compulsion.

Suppose that you kneel on the ground with an eight-week-old puppy and put him in heel position. He screams bloody murder but you continue to hold him there until he stops resisting. Then you tell him, "Good job!" That is a form of compulsion. If you use a tasty tidbit of food to lure a puppy into a sit, over a dogwalk or through a chute, that too is a form of

MAKING SENSE OF COMPULSION AND CORRECTION

When I get a new puppy, I teach him from an early age that there are basic rules he must obey. When he thoroughly understands what is wanted of him, yet he chooses not to comply because he has his own agenda (such as sniffing the ground or chasing a squirrel) I correct him—mildly, but nonetheless a correction. It does not matter that he is the cutest and most adorable puppy on the face of the earth. If I ask him to sit, he must sit. If I ask him to come, he must come. That is basic compliance. I instill the attitude that training is fun, but there are rules that must be followed. I never beg a puppy to compulsion training. Shaping behaviors with food, clickers, toys, or play is a form of compulsion. It is how we go about implementing the compulsion that makes the training pleasant or unpleasant. As conscientious trainers it is our responsibility to make training as interesting and enjoyable as possible for the puppy.

Handlers often run afoul in training by thinking, "My puppy's attitude is so wonderful, and I do not want to do anything to ruin it." So they offer their puppy absolutely no guidance or direction. Subsequently, the puppy quickly learns to do as he pleases. He becomes a little devil with his own agenda. The first time this puppy experiences any *compulsion* is during obedience training. Guess what the puppy is not going to like?

CORRECT THE RIGHT WAY

There are countless misconceptions regarding corrections. Let's set the record straight. First and foremost, the only time I would ever correct a very young puppy is if he is biting me or biting at another dog. He doesn't know anything yet. You cannot correct a puppy for doing something he doesn't know is wrong.

Several months ago the owner of a ten-week-old Labrador Retriever came to my puppy class. The first thing she said was, "He is so bad. He won't come when he's called!" If you had a six-month-old baby, what would you expect him to know? You certainly would not expect him to feed or dress himself, run his own bath, or change his own diaper. Yet handlers think nothing of expecting young puppies to behave like a well-trained adult dog. They are puppies! They are not born pre-trained as competition dogs. It is your job as a handler and trainer to instill the behaviors you want. How do you do it? Inch by inch by inch.

> **Correction is taking a behavior that is wrong and making it right.**

It is impossible to arbitrarily set an age when it is acceptable to correct a puppy. If and when you administer a correction should always depend on how thoroughly you have taught the exercise. Let's say, for example, you have a six- or seven-month-old puppy. You have been diligently working on the "come" exercise and you are sure that the puppy understands the command. Yet one day when you say "Fido, come," he decides to first check out a clump of leaves or an enticing aroma. In that situation, a small correction is warranted. Go over to him, give him a small collar shake and tell him, "Hey, I said come." Again, it's important to stress that this correction is given only when the puppy thoroughly understands the command and not a nanosecond sooner.

On the other hand, it doesn't matter if you have a six-month-old puppy or a three-year-old adult dog, if you have not first taught him to "come," then you cannot correct him for not coming. To do so is unfair, and it would undermine the foundation on which a trusting human/canine relationship is built.

Second, and equally important, the definition of a correction is to take a behavior that is wrong and make it right. It is that simple. A correction should never mean that a dog is bad—only that he did something wrong. You correct the wrong choice and make the right choice happen. For whatever reason, handlers often have a difficult time comprehending this concept. When administered properly a correction will not ruin a dog's attitude.

TO SUCCESS IN OBEDIENCE

- Strive to improve the overall communication between you and your dog by learning to give clear, concise and consistent verbal and signal cues.

- Focus on your puppy (or adult dog) one hundred percent of the time while training.

- Work at improving your timing when giving commands, praise or corrections.

- Maintain your dog's attention all of the time while in the ring.

- Think of the Novice, Open or Utility class exercises as one big exercise, not five or six individual ones.

- View your training as constantly striving to improve. Practice complete "run throughs" only occasionally to see how your training is coming along.

- Remember, there is no such thing as a bored dog; there are only boring trainers.

- Puppies grow into adult dogs that are products of what we put into them. Have a clear and concise picture of the behaviors you want in the ring and then strive to achieve it in a training environment.

- Continually strive to improve your training by practicing good training techniques. Avoid simply going through the motions.

- Think of your puppy as a clean slate. Then fill him with excellence!

A Welsh Terrier puppy learns to stop in the contact zone. Enthusiasm, reliability, and quick responses are taught at an early age by not allowing the puppy to ignore you. Photo courtesy Diane Bauman and Ali Roukas.

Corrections Must Be Unemotional

It is the physical or verbal *anger* that a handler puts into a correction that severs the lines of communication, demoralizes the dog, and ruins his attitude. Corrections should always be unemotional. Realistically, you could make substantial physical corrections on an adult dog and not affect his attitude as long as the corrections were done in a positive manner. (I am not advocating this policy. I am merely attempting to illustrate it is the negative emotions such as anger, frustration, and disappointment that affect a dog's attitude.) When a correction is given in anger, a dog, depending on his temperament, will respond with aggression or submission. He might try to escape from his handler or completely shut down. The dog is responding to the handler's emotions, not the correction itself.

Nagging Is Not Correction

If you make the same correction over and over again and the dog is not getting the message, you are nagging. Physical nagging, like verbal nagging, does not teach a puppy or adult dog anything positive. Physical nagging is when you make a correction that requires repetition. If you correct in the right way, your dog should immediately understand the wrong behavior and then execute the right behavior upon your request. Once the correct behavior is performed, you should praise the dog lavishly. "Good boy! That's what I wanted!"

Most dogs tend to avoid corrections. They might react to the correction, but if the timing is not correct they will not understand why it was given. When Bronco, my Border Collie, was six or seven months old, other handlers could not believe how responsive he was to my commands and they all wanted to know my secret. There really was no secret. From the time Bronco was eight weeks old I never allowed him to be unresponsive to my commands. If he was sniffing the ground, I would gently tweak him or do something silly to get his attention back on me. I simply never gave him the opportunity to develop bad habits.

You do not get enthusiasm, reliable responses, and understanding by using corrections. You get this type of response by teaching puppies at a very young age that they cannot ignore you, and by becoming the center of their universe.

61

Correct only when the puppy clearly understands what is expected, yet chooses not to comply. A correction given with wrong timing, wrong motives, or too much or too little force can ruin a dog's attitude toward performing.

Teach Before You Correct

Always teach first. If you correct a puppy that does not understand a command or that is confused or worried, he will fear you rather than trust you. A good rule of thumb is to encourage a puppy any time he is learning a new task, is confused, or is worried. When he has thoroughly mastered the task and has complete comprehension of what you want, yet he chooses not to comply, then it is fair to correct him.

Give corrections only for *major* infractions. As I mentioned earlier, the majority of a puppy's life should be about management, fostering his zany personality, and shaping and molding his character. You do this by instilling desired behaviors in a fun and positive environment. Help the puppy by praising, rewarding, and creating desired behaviors. Remember, it's much easier to create good habits than it is to go back and fix bad habits.

Know How and How Much to Correct

Like praise, what constitutes a correction is different for every dog. The amount of force your puppy needs will depend on his temperament. You should use enough force (and no more) that your puppy gets the message the first time. Then move on. Too much force will most assuredly scare or possibly even injure your puppy. A correction that is too light is tantamount to nagging. You will have to repeat the correction more than once before you get a response.

Shelties, as a general rule, tend to resent corrections. With my adult Shelties, if I change the tone of my voice ever so slightly or use their collar to give them a small correction, they may hold a grudge well into their senior years. At the opposite extreme, if I quickly pop the buckle collar on my Border Collies, they go wild. The quick collar pop gets them excited. As you gain experience as a trainer, you will find that the way each puppy reacts to a collar pop (or any other correction) depends upon his individual personality and temperament.

While my Border Collies love the playful collar pops, if I frown at them, they will try harder to please me. I probably could not hurt my German Shepherd physically (nor would I want to), but he can be crushed mentally if I scold him. The point is, what constitutes a correction for one puppy may not be objectionable to another. What would discourage a behavior in one puppy may actually encourage it in another.

That is why it is imperative that you learn to read your puppy and be flexible. Every dog is different. A six-month-old Welsh Terrier can easily maneuver weave poles, while a six-month-old Afghan will barely be able to negotiate a flight of stairs without tripping all over his feet. Would you correct the Afghan puppy for his inability to negotiate the weave poles? Never!

One of the keys to good training is knowing not just *how*, but also *when* to correct. Unfortunately, corrections seem to be the first line of defense for most handlers whenever things go wrong. In obedience training, anticipation on the recall or come exercise is often a problem. In the agility ring, jumping the gun at the start line or on the pause box is a similar situation. Let's say you have worked hard on the "stay" portion of the recall exercise. One day you turn your back (as if you are going to do a recall) and your ten-month-old puppy gets up, but then suddenly stops dead in his tracks. Most handlers will correct the puppy's act of getting up. They fail to realize that the puppy just had a proverbial "light bulb moment" and made a great decision. Anticipation is the best thing that can happen in training—it shows that learning has taken place and that the puppy has a desire to please you. By realizing that he had not yet been called, and then stopping, the puppy just demonstrated that he is learning. Never correct a puppy for anticipating. It will confuse and demoralize him. Instead, praise the puppy for the action of stopping and realizing that he had not yet been called. Tell him, "That was good," or "Aren't you clever! What a good job!" Always go back and work on reinforcing the weak areas, but *never correct anticipation.*

You can have the most magnificent puppy in the world, but if you are not proficient at reading his temperament, personality, quirks, and idiosyncrasies, and are not open-minded and willing to adapt your training methods to his individual character, you might as well take up tiddlywinks. Your chances of maximizing the puppy's potential are severely diminished. Furthermore, you must never allow your own ego to interfere with your puppy's training. Learn to recognize and accept when you have made a mistake in your training and quickly take the necessary steps to remedy the situation.

Every dog is an individual. If you want to be a good trainer, you must learn to read each individual dog's personality and adapt your training methods accordingly.

THE MIDAS TOUCH

The key to an effective correction is that it must be immediate and meaningful. The puppy should learn from it and need the correction only once to get the message. Then you move on. If you have ever observed a bitch with her babies, she is quite adept at making a correction with the precise amount of harshness necessary to make her point. Ninety-nine percent of the time the puppy gets the message the first time and the offensive behavior stops immediately. The mother rarely, if ever, under- or over-corrects her babies.

My corrections rarely consist of anything more than a verbal scolding or a combination of a verbal scolding and a scruff shaking. The key is catching the puppy *in the act* of the deed. Timing is critical. It does no good to correct a puppy after the fact. It is a total waste of time. You will only confuse him.

Let's say you are working on the sit-stay command with your six-month-old puppy. You give him the command and (because you have thoroughly reinforced the command while standing at his side) you are now ready to step directly in front of him. Things go as planned for about fifteen seconds. Then, suddenly, your puppy decides to stand up. Because he is still learning the exercise, a correction is not warranted. Simply put him back in the exact position he was when he broke his sit-stay and remind him to "stay." Of course, his training will be greatly enhanced if you can learn to read his body language and predict his behavior before it happens. Anticipating your puppy's behavior allows you to be proactive and make the necessary adjustments. That can be as simple as reminding him to "sit" or "stay."

If, however, you are working on the exact same exercise with a ten- or twelve-month-old puppy that thoroughly understands the exercise but decides to check out the pretty Poodle, then a correction is most definitely warranted. Walk calmly over to him, take hold of his buckle collar or scruff, and give him a firm (not harsh) shake. Ask him in no uncertain terms, "What are you doing over here? Knock it off." It is the tone of voice, not necessarily the choice of words, that helps to make the correction effective. Keep your voice calm yet firm and demanding, but never angry. Yelling, screaming, ranting or raving at your puppy is not a correction—it's a crime in progress. After you have made the correction, release the puppy and play with him for a few seconds. Then set him back in the original sit-stay position. Tell him, "That's your sit" and then walk away from him again.

> **Effective correction is immediate and meaningful.**

Points of Importance

First, it is critical that the correction be given while the puppy is in the incorrect position. It does not help if you take him back to where he was doing his "sit-stay" and correct him there. If you correct him while he is in the correct position, you will only confuse him. If you correct him while he is in the incorrect position and praise him when he is the proper position he will quickly learn right from wrong. You have given him clear and concise direction.

Second, it is essential that you release him and play with him after each correction. Playing takes his mind off the correction and allows him to get back in the right frame of mind in order to focus on the task before him. Throw his ball. Play a quick tug game. Ask him to speak or wave. Do whatever is necessary to restore him to a happy, eager-to-learn attitude. Never continue training until your puppy is happy and has forgotten the correction. Too often handlers make a big production out of a correction. Once again, remember the canine mother. Her corrections are clear, swift, and accurate, and she never prolongs the correction longer than necessary. Unfortunately, handlers can get so caught up in the act of correcting the puppy that they forget about releasing and playing with him. If you fail to restore your puppy's attitude after a correction and continue training while your puppy is in a poor frame of mind, you will inadvertently cause him to shut down. Eventually he will lose the desire to learn. Restoring his attitude, enthusiasm, and desire to train will then become a long, uphill road littered with potholes.

VERBAL CORRECTIONS

Verbal corrections are a source of spirited debate and contention among trainers. Personally, I am a firm believer that puppies, as well as adult dogs, seldom, if ever, learn from verbal corrections. For instance, you are working on the sit stay exercise and your puppy begins to sniff the ground. Yelling "No sniff!" from fifteen feet away will not teach your puppy anything positive. It is nothing more than a form of verbal nagging because most puppies will ignore the command. Subsequently, in a very short time your puppy will become indifferent to your voice.

That said, there are many situations such as in herding where dogs must learn to take verbal corrections from a distance. Years ago, Patrick Shannahan, one of the country's top stock dog trainers, told me, "Before you get your dog out to work you'd better have your running boots on because there will be many times when you will need to cover 400 yards in order to reinforce a verbal correction." Oh how right he was! For instance, if my dog is coming up too fast on the sheep or is a bit pushy, I call out

If you are training your puppy and another dog is barking and carrying on, do not, under any circumstances, yell at the barking dog or tell him to "Knock it off." Your puppy will be unable to comprehend that you are yelling at a completely different dog. Instead, he will think you are scolding him, and his attitude will suffer. This is especially detrimental to a puppy that tends to be wimpy, worried, or apprehensive.

"Easy!" or "Lie down!" If he does not respond, I take off running and cover every inch of distance between us—some days it might be 50 yards, other days it might be 400 yards—and make him respond. I tell him, "What do you think you're doing? I told you 'Easy!'" I never give multiple requests. That is where trainers often run amuck with verbal corrections.

Remember, always teach first, and do it while the puppy is within a two- or three-foot radius of you. When the puppy thoroughly understands the command, gradually begin adding distractions and distance (see Block 8). Do not attempt to teach the basics (including verbal corrections) while the dog is halfway across a field and focused on sheep. This is one of the reasons why I never work my dogs on stock in a field until they are at least ten months old. I want a puppy to develop *reliable* responses to basic commands such as "down" and "come" before I put him on stock. Then, when I give him a verbal command or correction from 10 yards or 400 yards away, he will respond.

Many handlers let their three- or four-month-old puppies run around and chase stock. "Look at him! He's already working stock at twelve weeks!"

An adult Border Collie eagerly and enthusiastically follows his owner's command. Photo Courtesy of Bobbie Anderson.

This young puppy is being introduced to ducks in a small, enclosed area. The puppy should respond to the "come" command and should not be allowed to chase the ducks uncontrolled. Photo © Anita Paull.

I am not a proponent of this type of training. Livestock is highly unpredictable, and a three- or even six-month-old puppy is at high risk for injury. The young puppy has not developed the necessary reflexes and speed needed to get out of a dangerous situation. When a puppy is about ten months old and responding reliably to commands, then I start him on stock. At first we work in a small pen so that I can get between him and the stock if necessary.

REINFORCEMENT

Patty Ruzzo, a top obedience trainer, always says, "Behavior that is not reinforced will extinguish." All trainers should commit this ideology to memory! For instance, my three-year-old Border Collie thoroughly understands the "lie down" command. However, I continue to reinforce the behavior by telling him "Good down!" or "Good job!" When I say "Bronco, down!" I immediately take a step toward him and also give him the hand signal for "down" to reinforce the behavior. I might toss a tidbit of food or a toy toward him as reinforcement. Another time I might run past Bronco, tap him, and tell him "Good down!" I never put him in a position where he can develop sloppy or slow responses. If I tell him "lie down" from 200 yards away and he complies, I will run out to him, pat him on the shoulders and tell him "Yea! Look at you! That was an excellent down!" (Of course, I don't run 200 yards every single time I tell him "down," but I do make a point of reinforcing the behaviors I want.) If you want your dog to respond consistently and reliably to your commands, you must continue to reinforce desired behaviors throughout the dog's working life.

Maximize your training by practicing precision, and continue to reinforce correct behavior.

THE END MUST JUSTIFY THE MEANS

It is important that you understand why you are utilizing a particular training method or correction. Try looking at the correction from your puppy's point of view. That should give you a pretty good indication of what will and will not work.

Furthermore, try not to fall into the trap of making a correction because you saw someone else do it. I have seen top handlers jerk a young dog off his feet because he broke a sit-stay, or slam an adolescent dog on the ground when he

The ring should always be a positive experience for both puppies and peewee handlers.

Conformation classes should be fun. This six-month-old Rottweiler receives a treat and encouragement during her first show. Photo by B. J. McKinney.

refused a "down" command. Sure, they got the results they wanted, but at what cost? The end does not necessarily justify the means. Perhaps it is best explained in the words of Sylvia Bishop, England's expert and foremost authority on canine training and behavior: "It is very easy to train a dog by total domination, that is by using a check chain and force; but whilst this produces results it does not produce the keenness or what I always refer to as 'the want.'"

With the exception of the puppy classes in the conformation ring, there are few instances when a puppy would be in the ring. However, too often handlers are overly anxious to set their junior dog (i.e., eight or ten months old) up for a correction. There is an enormous difference between training, proofing or fixing a problem in a training situation, and intentionally setting a young dog up. Nothing boils my blood faster than hearing a handler say, "I can't wait to take him to a fun match and set him up so I can really nail him." This shameful practice only instills distrust. If your puppy cannot rely on you, the fundamental ingredient in the human/canine relationship is lost. When you begin showing competitively and the going gets tough, your dog will quit on you, because he will associate the show ring with being corrected.

Without exception, the ring should always, always, always be a positive experience for your puppy or adult dog. If you take him to a fun match and set him up to make a correction while he's in the ring, the ring is no longer a fun place to be. Think about it.

A correction, given with proper force and proper timing, extinguishes wrong behavior. A correction given with wrong timing, wrong motives, or with too much or too little force, can ruin a dog's attitude toward performing. Learning to use compulsion and correction effectively is one of the distinguishing factors between a mediocre trainer and an excellent one.

DITTO—WHEN NERVES COLLIDE

Every puppy presents unique training challenges. Some puppies are more challenging than others, but all dogs have quirks and peculiarities that are guaranteed to pop up in training or competition.

My Border Collie, Ditto, is no exception. Ditto was eleven weeks old when I brought him home. Despite his intelligence, loving personality and tremendous heart, Ditto was nothing short of a challenge when it came to training. He loved to play, but as soon as I said, "Let's go train," his tail would tuck between his legs, his head would drop, and he would slink to the building as if he was being led to his death.

The real problem with Ditto was that he did not like to be wrong, so learning new commands or exercises worried him. The stress of being around stock or learning new exercises would cause him to avoid the situation. The saving grace was that Ditto kept coming back when I asked him for more. Equally important, I never allowed him to quit on me.

If he became frightened and tried to run away I would call him back and he would try it again. He would always hang in there and keep trying. Once he successfully learned a behavior he was happy and willing to comply in either a training or competitive environment. When Ditto made a mistake, I never made a big deal about it. I simply said, "Oh well, let's do it again."

This type of canine personality takes an enormous amount of energy and patience because you must constantly behave as if nothing is wrong. One of the biggest mistakes you can make is to buy into your puppy's fear. "Oh, you poor little thing. You don't like to train? Come here, Mommy will make it better." The puppy is thinking, "I'm so glad she finally understands. Now I can go back to being in control and doing what I want."

Ditto grew into a successful and competitive dog that excelled in obedience and herding. He was incredibly bright and social. He loved the show atmosphere because he understood his job. I never entered him in a competition until he was solid on his exercises. He retired at five years old with an Obedience Trial Championship Title (OTCH), two 200-scores and over fifteen High in Trials. He spent one year of his competitive career on the sidelines recovering from shoulder surgery.

Here are some puppy training tips that helped me to work through Ditto's worrisome personality:

- Be patient. Understand that this type of personality takes longer to train. Let your dog work through his fear period in a positive environment.

- Do not get bogged down in his attitude. His attitude and speed will come back after he works through the problem.

- Be demanding but fair and consistent. Do not browbeat your puppy into learning. This will render him helpless.

- Learn to ignore your puppy's behaviors when he worries or wants to quit.

- Never allow him to quit on his own. Persevere. Work through the problem.

- Always finish on a positive note.

- Always maintain an upbeat attitude that conveys to the puppy, "This is fun." Do not buy into your dog's phobia.

Bobbie Anderson scoring a perfect 200 and High in Trial with her Border Collie, OTCH Redtop Double Play UDX, "Ditto."

Block Six: Maximize Drive

IN ITS SIMPLEST FORM, PREY DRIVE REFERS to the natural hunting, killing, chasing, and retrieving instincts a puppy inherits from his ancestors. When a Border Collie stares intently at stock, herds the vacuum cleaner, or nips and chases the neighborhood kids, he is displaying the qualities of a genetically inherited prey drive. When a working retriever enthusiastically dives into icy water and brings a downed bird to hand, or a terrier goes to ground, these, too, are examples of prey drive.

HIGH PREY DRIVE EQUALS HIGH ENERGY

Many of the herding breeds, primarily Border Collies, have become popular in all areas of canine competition because they are fun, fast, high-energy dogs. Experienced handlers make training and showing them look like a walk in the park. These dogs tend to have the naturally high prey drives and abundant reserves of energy and endurance necessary for the job for which they were originally bred.

Yet high-prey-drive or high-energy dogs are often misunderstood. There is a colossal difference between high-energy and hyperactive puppies. High-energy puppies are like sponges—they love to learn and interact with their owners, and they truly relish a challenge. Mental stimulation is as important to a high-energy puppy as is physical activity.

Furthermore, high-prey-drive puppies have a tremendous work ethic that makes showing and training them an absolute thrill. A high-drive puppy coupled with the right handler can become a magnificent competition team. It is invigorating to train and show a high-prey-drive dog because his personality does not require him to be constantly coaxed or cheerled. When properly trained, a high-drive puppy will grow into an adult dog that will consistently be there for you when the going gets tough in a competitive environment.

I work with mostly high-prey-drive breeds because my own personality bends more toward high energy. Every handler needs to scrutinize their own personality to determine whether a high- or low-prey-drive puppy best suits them.

At the opposite end of the scale, the hyperactive puppy's energy is more scattered. He may go a hundred miles per hour all day long, yet he can rarely focus on any task for more than a minute. The hyperactive puppy will make you curse the day you became involved in the sport of dogs.

MANAGING A HIGH-DRIVE PUPPY

High-drive and high-energy puppies are not without problems either. Handlers can inadvertently wade hip deep into trouble by thinking a turbo-charged or "up" puppy will magically solve their training problems. Sorry, folks, a high-drive or high-energy puppy does not mean you get to sit back on your laurels while your puppy does all the work. Quite the opposite, in fact. To successfully channel the abundant energy of a high-drive puppy, you must be intensely inviting, stimulating, and exciting. Otherwise you will end up with a stressed dog. As an owner-handler of a high-drive puppy you must be proficient at tuning in to him and reading him when he is a baby. You must remain two steps ahead of him at all times or you can quickly and inadvertently re-linquish your position of control. You must give your puppy the impression that you are on top of every situation. High-drive dogs must understand that while you work together as a team, you will call the shots. Someone once said that high-prey-drive puppies have such an acute mental discernment and keen practical sense that they can easily "pick your pockets clean and leave you smiling about it."

Don't forget to take your vitamins—you will need them. High-energy puppies just love to be included in every activity, so it's imperative that you incorporate them into your day-to-day routines like walking, swimming or simply running errands. Older puppies can accompany you as you jog or ride a bicycle. All this activity can be daunting if you are already struggling to find

High-drive puppies and adult dogs, such as Border Collies, are often misunderstood.

Decide if you are most suited to a high- or low-energy dog.

High-energy dogs like to be included in your day-to-day activities. Swimming and retrieving are great outlets for their abundant energy.

the requisite time to balance family and work.

Handlers often want a high-drive puppy for training and showing but they fail to understand that they also have to live with this puppy twenty-four hours a day. Consequently they get frustrated and upset with the puppy because he has a short attention span, anticipates commands, digs holes in the yard, barks incessantly, cannot settle down in the house, shows aggression with other dogs, and is constantly distracted. Training a high-drive puppy for thirty minutes once a day and then confining him to a kennel for the next twenty-three hours does not come close to meeting his energy needs. Behavior problems are inevitable when high-energy puppies do not have acceptable physical and mental outlets for their excess energy.

A huge percentage of people who get a high-drive puppy (or adult dog) try to suppress or dominate him. Rather than learning to channel and control the energy, they promptly try to squash the dog's enthusiasm. Dogs—especially Border Collies—that are genetically driven to perform a specific task are so intelligent that they truly resent being dominated and eventually will rebel.

In addition to training, high-energy puppies love learning challenging tricks to keep them mentally stimulated. Teach your puppy to wave, stick out his tongue, close his mouth, bark on command, roll over, play dead, or walk sideways. In a competitive environment these fun tricks can be subtly used whenever you think he is about to get himself into trouble. Perhaps it's at the start line in agility or as you move from one exercise to another in the obedience ring. You can, for example, give him a subtle command such as "close your mouth" to work on as you move from one exercise to another. A simple mental trick will give your high-drive dog's brain something to think about. If his brain is focused, he will be less likely to

Mental stimulation is equally as important as physical stimulation for the high-energy dog.

anticipate the next command. Ten or fifteen seconds in between exercises can seem like a lifetime to a high-energy dog.

In addition to tricks, I give each of my dogs a daily responsibility to help stimulate their minds. For instance, after I have fed the dogs, my Border Collie, Rio, loves to run around and gather up all the dog dishes out of the crates. My Sheltie, Cajun, and my English Cocker, Raider, love to carry the mail in every day and they are very possessive about their job. Nike, my German Shepherd, gathers up all the dog bones and toys off the dog room floor before I vacuum. These activities might seem inconsequential, yet it's one more avenue to mentally stimulate my dogs. Dogs that are included as important members of the family seldom have a reason to feel stressed.

On a final note, high-drive and high-energy puppies need to know the rules. They need guidance and direction in their lives. The stressed, depressed, and obnoxious puppies are the ones

Hide-and-seek games arouse a puppy's competitive spirit. Duck behind a building or tree as you call your puppy's name enthusiastically. When he finds you, lavish him with praise and tasty tidbits of food.

that do not clearly understand there are household rules to which they must adhere. If these puppies do not feel obligated to obey day-to-day household rules, they generally grow into adult dogs that are not very committed to obedience training.

INCREASING LOW PREY DRIVE

If you have a puppy with a low prey drive, or that is submissive, subdued, and reluctant to play, do not despair. All of the games and techniques illustrated in "Block Two: Make Training Fun" will help to increase a puppy's play or prey drive. Also, if your puppy has a very low play drive or is apprehensive about playing, do not worry about incorporating specific exercises or commands into the play. Rather, focus on building his excitement and enthusiasm about being with you and being comfortable playing with different toys. This can take anywhere from a few days to several months. It depends on the puppy's temperament and personality. However, when he starts to relax, he will start to play, and when he starts to play he will be more receptive to learning.

Most puppies have a natural predatory or chase instinct. Generally speaking, the herding, hound, and terrier breeds are easily stimulated by moving objects—a cat, sheep, squirrel, or a favorite toy attached to a string. A puppy's natural desire to chase is easily activated as long as an object is moving. The key to instilling a strong prey or chase instinct is to always, always, always move *away* from your puppy. Some ingrained habits are hard to break, and this seems to be one of the hardest for many handlers. For whatever reason, handlers have a natural propensity to move in to their puppy. The goal is to get your puppy to chase you or an object being dragged on the floor. It is virtually impossible to build

High-drive dogs need stimulation, mental challenges, responsibility, and enforced guidelines.

a strong chase instinct if you are moving toward your puppy.

If you have a breed that is less inclined to chasing and stalking, building a strong chase instinct will take some serious energy on your part. However, inciting or building a puppy's chase instinct is fundamental to creating a strong play or prey drive. The time you spend building strong drives will come back tenfold as your puppy grows bigger and bolder and begins to endure the rigors of training and eventually campaigning.

I play lots of chase and hide-and-seek games to arouse my puppy's competitive spirit. If I am walking in the yard, for example, I might suddenly take off running and encourage my puppy to chase me by enthusiastically saying his name and clapping my hands. Or I might hide behind a bush or a tree and encourage him to "find me." If I am in the house, I might (without warning) take off running down the hallway as I say my puppy's name enthusiastically. When he "finds me," I praise him lavishly. I tell him "Aren't you clever! You found your mom!" If the puppy looks away, I might duck behind a chair and say his name in a happy, cheerful tone of voice. Again, when he "finds me" I get on the floor and roll around with him as I praise him lavishly: "Aren't you smart!" or "Look at you!" I might throw a toy and try to beat him to it. All of these behaviors are done in a very informal atmosphere. They are spontaneous games overflowing with tons of excitement. I am not only building a strong play and prey drive, I am endearing myself as my puppy's primary source of fun. I am the only person who takes him to see sheep, go swimming, play ball and so forth. He associates me with all of the fun things in his life.

I use a lot of variations in my tone of voice to feed my puppy's ego and make him feel like a million bucks. Sometimes I growl and bark at him

THE IMPORTANCE OF

Drive is wonderful. Drive makes training and showing easier. Drive is important, but the desire to please is more important. You can have a ton of drive but if your dog has no desire to please you, you've got zip. All the drive in the world won't help you if your dog doesn't want to please you or be with you. The dog needs heart and desire. If you have desire *and* drive, you will go farther.

Hound puppies like this Whippet have a natural prey drive that is easily stimulated by a moving object. Photo by Judith Strom.

while we are playing. The noise helps to pique his curiosity and keep his focus on me. It is playful and exciting and helps to encourage interaction. If he barks, I tell him, "Good one!" or "Good bark!" This helps to build confidence. If he is confident, he feels good about himself. If he has a bit of a wimpy personality, I reinforce the behaviors I want by telling him he is "Clever." If he jumps in the air, I tell him, "Good jump!" or "Brilliant!" The more I can boost his ego, the more confident he will feel. He may even begin to think he is clever.

USING PLAY TO INCREASE DRIVE

You can provoke play in a puppy with low prey drive by slightly aggravating him. No doubt you have watched a puppy trying to entice an adult dog to play. Generally the puppy nips or barks at the adult dog, then quickly runs away as if taunting the adult to chase and play with him. Simulate the same type of behavior to encourage your puppy to interact and play with you. Start by gently and playfully prodding or poking at your puppy and then moving away from him. Running away will help to incite his chase instinct and encourage him to play. If your puppy is on a six-foot leash or longline, he will have no choice but to follow when you run. Again, you can try growling, barking, yipping or making funny noises as you gently pinch him. I slip my right hand into the buckle collar and my left hand under the puppy's belly. Then I pick him a few inches off the ground, spin him around once and quickly put him back on the ground. As soon as his little feet hit the ground I take off running and encourage him to follow.

The more you keep a puppy from playing, the more he will want to play.

In the beginning, if your puppy is worried or uncertain, he might try to run away from you. His lack of confidence will inhibit him from responding to your encouragement. His timidness or sense of insecurity will cause his flight instinct to kick in. It is important that you do not allow him to leave or run away from you. Use the leash to continue encouraging him to play and to keep him close to you. If you accidentally step on his foot and he screams, do not baby him. This will only reinforce his submissive behavior. Try not to treat him like a piece of china. Rather, tell him "Good scream!" and continue playing until you get some semblance of a positive response from him. Remember, if you treat him like a zombie, he will act like a zombie. If you are as dull as a post, your puppy will be dull too.

Pick Me

You can increase your puppy's low play drive and arouse his competitive spirit by tethering him to a nearby tree or a ground stake or confining him while you play with or train another dog. (Always use a buckle collar, *never* a choke chain or pinch collar.) If you have a multiple-dog household, you have probably witnessed the same results when you take one dog out to train. More than likely the other dogs will jump, bark and yip as if to say, "Pick me! Pick me!" You can stimulate the same behavior to arouse your puppy's competitive spirit by temporarily limiting his participation but not his view of the fun and games. Puppies are naturally inquisitive. The more you keep them from playing, the more they will want to play.

Last but not least, if a puppy is not enthusiastic or interested in playing, put him in his crate or exercise pen for several hours. When he has spent some time alone and his desire for human interaction or play is at it's greatest, take him out and try playing with him again.

All of these behaviors help to engage and entice your puppy to play and subsequently build a strong play or prey drive. If any of your behaviors elicit a response, praise your puppy immediately. Think about the old Chinese proverb, "A journey of a thousand miles begins with a single step." By praising even the tiniest response from your puppy, you systematically begin building his prey drive. Look for results in small increments and then build upon those results. Most importantly, remember that your puppy is an individual complete with his own personality, talents, quirks, idiosyncrasies, and limitations. If you are committed you can build stronger play and prey drives, but always keep in mind your puppy's individual qualities. Just because he is a Golden Retriever does not mean he will naturally love training.

Food and Toys

A common misconception about food and play drives is that if your dog has one of them you will not need the other. If you like having options in your training, work on instilling all of the drives (e.g., play, prey, food, retrieve). You never know when you might need to use one rather than another.

For instance, my Border Collies do not care about food when there are toys around. They much prefer to interact with me via play. I can whip them into a frenzy simply by producing a toy or ball. The problem with this is they are so fixated and intense about the toys that the exercise we are working on becomes secondary. To counter this I often use scrumptious tidbits of food as a reward (rather than a toy). That helps the dog focus more on what I want instead of being obsessed about a toy. It also helps to calm him and make him think about the task at hand.

BUILDING PLAY DRIVE

Here are some tips to help you develop a strong play drive in your dog.

- Persevere. It takes a lot of energy to get a dog to play when he's interested in food. The long-term results are well worth the effort.

- On occasion, try doing all of your play training at the beginning of a training session. Food train for the last half of the session. Always end on a positive note.

- If your puppy quits when you bring out a toy, do not make the mistake of going back to the food. Guess who is controlling the situation!

- If your puppy is reluctant to play, don't worry about training exercises. Focus on playing. When he relaxes, his attitude will be more conducive to learning.

- Have a clear picture in your mind of the exercise or behavior you are attempting to teach. Strive to achieve it in a training situation.

My Sheltie, Cajun, has an extremely high food drive. Food is very important to him. I do not want to discourage that behavior. However, I also want him to work when there is no food forthcoming, and I definitely want play to be important to him. So, with Cajun, I continually need to work at instilling a solid play drive and making play fun.

Some puppies are not motivated by either food or play. To increase a puppy's food drive, always train and play while he has an empty stomach. Use mouth-watering, irresistible tidbits of foods like chicken, boiled heart, steak, cheese, tortellini, or liverwurst. Make the reward worth working for. Let's say someone offered you $1 to bathe their puppy. Would you do it? The motivation is minuscule. If they offered you $100 to bathe the same puppy, would you reconsider? The motivation has increased significantly. If you want results, train your puppy with $100 bills (figuratively speaking). Boiled liver is a $100 bill. Your puppy's everyday crunchy dog food is a $1 bill. As they say when fishing, "If the fish are not biting—change the bait."

You should also vary the kinds of food from day to day, and occasionally from exercise to exercise, as a means of spurring your puppy's motivation. Use chicken one day and steak the next. Or, use turkey wieners for the cookie toss game and liverwurst to teach the go-out exercise. Mix it up. Keep it interesting.

Another trick is to hide some tasty tidbits of food in your puppy's toy in order to stimulate curiosity. When the puppy shows the slightest interest in the toy, praise him and give him the food hidden in it.

THE RETRIEVE DRIVE

The retrieve drive is like any other drive; some puppies have naturally high retrieve drives while others need channeled persuasion in order to flourish. Many of the games introduced in Block One are perfect for setting the foundation for a strong retrieve drive. Retrieving games and exercises should not be played while a puppy is teething, however.

How to Develop a Strong Retrieve Drive

You build a strong retrieve drive the same way as any other drive—make it a fun game for the puppy. For instance, throw a ball and have the puppy chase after it. When he brings it back, rather than stand in one spot, generate excitement by clapping your hands and running to the opposite side of the yard or building. When he gets to you, praise him and allow him to strut around savoring his victory. Sometimes I will throw the ball and let it bounce off the wall before sending the puppy after it. The noise and fluctuation in the game helps to generate excitement.

If a puppy tends to be a bit indifferent about retrieving, throw a toy across the room and hold on to his leash as you both run for it. Make sure to get the toy. Tell him, "Too slow! I got it!" Dance around with the toy for a few seconds, clearly savoring your victory. Then throw it again and try to beat him to it. If he's slow, grab the toy again and tell him, "I got it! You're too slow!" After a few tries you should see some increase in your puppy's speed and enthusiasm. If he is trying exceptionally hard, race him to the toy but let him get it. Tell him, "Look at you! You got it. You're too fast!" Let him strut around and revel in his victory. Any type of praise is great as it helps to feed his ego and increase his drive.

When the puppy is a little older and can do a sit-stay, you can tell him to sit,

Step one: *To build speed and enthusiasm on retrieves, put your puppy on a leash or longline. Let him see you throw his toy. Hold him back slightly as you ask him, "Do you want to get it?"*

Step two: *Beat him to the toy as you both run for it.*

Step three: *Repeat the exercise, but this time let your puppy get the toy. Reward him with plenty of praise.*

Step one: Put your puppy on a "sit-stay" and walk halfway between him and his toy. Remind him in a fun voice, "Don't you cheat."

Step two: Tell your puppy "Get it" as you both run for the toy.

If your puppy gets the toy, grab his leash, pop him around to face you, and interact in a game of tug.

then throw his toy across the room. Remind him to sit as you walk toward the toy. When you have taken three or four steps, turn and tell him in a happy voice, "Don't you cheat!" Walk a few more steps and tell him again, "Don't you cheat. I'm watching you!" When about midway to the toy, tell him "Get it" as you both run for the toy. Make

sure you grab the toy on the fly and keep running around the building or yard waving it. Finally, play with the puppy for a minute, and then repeat.

A variation on this game is to have someone hold your puppy as you show him a toy or tasty tidbit of food. Let him see you throw the toy or food halfway across the room. While the person is still holding your puppy, run and grab the food or toy. Just as you grab it, the person holding the puppy lets go of him. Once you have grabbed the food, keep on running and when your puppy gets to you, throw the food or toy between your legs and let him get it. Praise him lavishly.

Another way to build speed and enthusiasm is to throw the puppy's toy and send him for it. As he picks it up and heads back to you, squat down and tap the floor. Tell him "Hurry, hurry, hurry" or "Run, run, run!" When he gets to you, shower him with kisses and plenty of praise. Lie flat on the ground and let him climb up on your tummy as you continue to lavish him with kisses. If he drops his toy, snatch it up, roll over on your tummy and hide the toy. Ask him, "Where'd it go?" If he looks away, tap him on the foot with the toy and then quickly hide it under your body again. Encourage him to root around and find the toy underneath your torso. When he finds it, throw the toy across the room and tell him to "Get it."

You can try throwing the toy across the room and send him for it with a "get it" or "take it" command. When he gets the toy and heads back toward you, turn your back to him, bend over and peek between your legs at him. Encourage him to run between your legs with his toy. The two of you can then interact in a tug game for a minute or two.

Another way that I build a puppy's enthusiasm for retrieving is to attach his obedience dumbbell or a toy to a light-weight string and systematically build excitement by dragging it on the floor. Of course, you will need to interject some excitement into the "game" rather than simply dragging the dumbbell or toy on the ground and hoping your puppy finds that behavior stimulating. Make the dumbbell or toy suddenly appear out of nowhere! Tell your puppy, "Ooooh, look what I've got!" Run

If your puppy drops his toy while you're playing, grab it, get on the floor, roll over on your tummy and encourage him to root around for it by asking him "Where's your toy?" Photo by JoAnne Carson.

across the room dragging the toy. When the puppy begins showing the slightest sign of interest in the toy, quickly snatch it up and say, "It's mine!" Hide it behind your back or hold it over your head. Ask, "Where did it go?" Puppies always want what they cannot have. Sit on the floor and drag the toy around you, or between your legs. In order to maximize the puppy's excitement and curiosity, do not allow him to get the toy until after his enthusiasm and excitement have piqued. Only at that time does he actually get to "capture" the toy.

TEACHING THE RETRIEVE

When I get a new puppy, regardless of whether he is eight weeks or eight months old, I start right away teaching him how to retrieve, and to enjoy retrieving. Like any other exercise, I make it a fun game. He also learns early on to retrieve a variety of items, such as stuffed toys, Frisbees®, balls, dumbbells, an eight-inch section of rubber hose, gloves, field dummies and so forth.

I begin by generating excitement. I drag or tap a toy on the ground and encourage my puppy to try and get it. Normally it takes only one or two minutes to rev him up. Once he's excited and eager to play, I move right into the steps below.

With Small Breed Or Young Puppies:

Step one: Hold the puppy a few inches off the ground. Let him see you toss the toy about ten feet in front of him. Talk to him. "What's that? Do you want to get it?"

Step two: Gently drop the puppy in a forward motion toward the toy.

Step three: Encourage him with a "Get it!" command. When the puppy gets the toy, praise him, "Good boy!" or "Look at you!" Back up as you encourage the puppy to bring the toy back. Allow him to strut around and savor his mammoth achievement. Gently tap him on the shoulder or hind end and ask him, "What have you got?" or "Ohhh, look at that pretty toy."

Step four: Interact in a game of tug before repeating the "game." Remember it is a game. It should be fun and exciting. All photos © Lana Young Photography.

With Older Puppies:

As your puppy matures and becomes more proficient at retrieving, try these steps:

- Gradually begin increasing the distance you throw the toy. To generate speed and excitement, toss the toy, send the puppy, and then run to the other side of the building. Clap your hands or say his name. When he returns with the toy, praise him lavishly. Allow him to strut around and savor his achievement.

- Begin adding small distractions. Throw the toy or dumbbell under the dining room table, or up the stairs. Toss it next to a bush or under a tree. Use your imagination to generate excitement and stimulate his brain.

- To encourage a strong hold, do a fun play retrieve; when he brings it back, put your hands on the toy while it is in his mouth. If he bites down or pulls back with the toy, release, clap your hands, and tell him, "Good hold" or "Strong puppy!"

- If he drops the toy, kick it across the room and race him to it. Encourage him with, "Get it!" or "Take it."

- While the toy is in his mouth, put one hand on his chest and one hand on the toy. Pretend to pull the toy really hard as you tell him, "You're too strong!" or "Strong boy!" This helps to build confidence and a stronger hold.

- A fun Sylvia Bishop game that can be played with a larger or older puppy: Put a chair in the center of the room. Hold your puppy's leash in one hand, the toy or dumbbell in the other. Run around the chair while encouraging your puppy to follow. As you circle the chair several times tell your puppy, "Get it. Get it. Get it." As you are circling, put the dumbbell on the edge of the chair and tell him "Take it." Praise lavishly when he picks it up.

- To teach a clean pick up, throw the dumbbell or toy into a corner. Send your puppy into the corner to get it. This technique prevents the puppy from circling the dumbbell or toy before picking it up.

Resistance training is an excellent "game" for building drive, desire, and enthusiasm.

Using Resistance to Increase Retrieve Drive

Do you remember the sibling roughhousing the youngest or smallest kids were always subjected to when you were a youngster walking home from school? You would try to race your siblings home, but one of them would grab the back of your jacket or sweater to keep you from moving forward. The tighter their grasp, the harder you worked at driving forward to break loose. When they finally let go of your jacket, the sudden lack of resistance propelled you forward.

Resistance training is a similar concept. Perhaps the most easily identifiable form of canine resistance training is sled dog racing. A portion of training sled dogs involves teaching a dog to pull against a consistent load. The handler holds the dogs back from their natural maximum speed in order to induce a stronger drive. Similar concepts can encourage and build both speed and desire in retrieving and recall exercises. The techniques vary slightly, but the outcome is basically the same. The goal is to use resistance to induce greater enthusiasm and strong drive.

Start by having your puppy on a six-foot leash. Throw an obedience dumbbell, field dummy, or toy across the yard. Spark your puppy's enthusiasm and motivation by holding him back as you throw the dumbbell or toy. Ask him in an exciting voice, "Do you want to get it?" Let your puppy go but continue holding on to his leash. Your body weight will provide a natural resistance as he pulls you across the yard toward his toy. The resistance the puppy feels as he leans into his collar will enhance his natural desire to drive forward.

In my experience, it is imperative that you lean back, keep both hands on the leash and keep it in line with the back of the puppy's head while you are running. Otherwise you will end up going head-over-tea-kettle as your puppy becomes more determined at charging for his toy. As your puppy grows older, you can increase his drive by slowing down. The slower you go, the harder he will have to dig in as he drives toward the toy.

A variation on the game that I like to use on my Border Collies is to teach them to lay into their collar. Again, it is the resistance they feel as they lay into their collar that provokes enthusiasm and induces a strong desire to drive forward. The only difference between this game and the above game is that my puppy is not pulling me across the yard. (I do, however, integrate both games into my puppy training and playing.) I start by winding up my puppy. When he is excited about his toy, I provide resistance by holding on to his collar as I throw the toy (or dumbbell). I play growl and tap him on his chest as I ask him in an exciting voice, "Do you want to get it?" Remember, when a puppy thinks he cannot have a toy, he will want it all the more. When I let go of him the sudden lack of resistance is going to propel him forward toward the toy. As a puppy grows stronger, his excitement will become so intense that he will literally stand on his hind feet and lay into his collar as I throw his dumbbell or toy.

With very young puppies—eight or ten weeks old—or very small breed puppies, you should alter the resistance game slightly. Hold the puppy under his tummy and lift him two or three inches off the ground. Let him see you toss his toy and encourage him by growling, "Rrrrrrrrrr," or by asking him, "Do you want to get it?" Most of the time his feet will start going a million miles an hour as he tries to squirm out of your grasp. *Gently* drop him in a forward motion to encourage him to go after the toy. When he gets it, quickly pop him back in your direction to get his attention back on you.

An adult dog lays into his collar on the retrieve as a form of resistance training.

Step one: When utilizing resistance training on a very young or small breed puppy, hold him a few inches off the ground. Let him see you toss his toy a few feet in front of you.

Step two: Encourage him to "get it" by growling at him, "Grrrrrrr," and asking him "Do you want to get it?" as you gently drop him in a forward motion.

Step three: When he gets his toy, use the leash to quickly yet gently pop him in your direction. Praise him with "Good boy!" The play collar pop gets your puppy's attention back on you.

Block Seven: Laying the Groundwork

IN THE WORDS OF GREEK PHILOSOPHER Aristotle, "What we have to learn to do, we learn by doing." Some 2,300 years later, we can still learn from his advice. Puppies learn through association, repetition, and consistency. Spend two or three minutes several times a day training him and it's remarkable how quickly a young puppy will progress.

With a new puppy, regardless of whether he is eight weeks or eight months old, I start right away laying the groundwork. I want to instill all of the behaviors that the puppy will need in order to successfully compete in a wide variety of canine events. That includes cultivating specific drives (play, prey, food, retrieve), teaching the basics (name recognition, come when called, various commands, how to take food nicely, follow me, find me), and using play to instill specific behaviors important in performance events (speed, enthusiasm, focus and attention). Of course, I always take into consideration a puppy's temperament and personality. Also, I proceed at a pace that is suitable for the mental and physical development of each individual puppy.

USING PLAY TO BUILD SPEED AND ENTHUSIASM

Diane Bauman, one of the top agility handlers in the country, is constantly asked how she gets her Cocker Spaniel to run so fast. The answer, according to Bauman, is that she never slows down the dog. Bauman is fond of saying, "There is no such thing as dogs that are too fast—only dogs that will not stop or handlers who cannot get to the right place at the right time."

Unfortunately, a handler inadvertently can slow a fast puppy because of his own sense of concern. For example, the handler worries that the puppy will fall off a seesaw or dog walk, so they tell the puppy, "Easy." They might give a "wait" command too early, which often creates anxiety and caution in a puppy. These behaviors normally will not manifest if the handler simply lets the puppy maneuver the obstacles at his own pace. If an eight-week-old puppy wants to gallop across a dog walk or a seesaw, let him gallop. The equipment should never be more than seven or eight inches off the ground, making it completely safe. The puppy should learn to stop in the contact area. However, he should never intentionally be slowed.

Fast dogs are born, not made. If your puppy is fast, don't try to slow him down. Just lower the obstacles so that they are safe for him. This three-month-old Afghan is learning the hand signal to jump.
Photo courtesy of Diane Bauman.

To speed up your puppy, speed up yourself!

One of the best methods for speeding up your puppy is to speed up yourself! Remember if you are slow and methodical, your puppy will eventually become slow and methodical.

I think it's important to note that fast dogs are born, not made. Yes, there are plenty of exercises and chase games you can play to increase your puppy's speed. However, there is a point when you must accept your puppy's limitations. If a magic formula for increasing speed existed, everyone would have a fast dog. You can improve your dog's performance, but you cannot turn him into a whiz kid if he does not have the genes. Years ago I bought a wonderful English Cocker puppy to show in obedience. Tang, as we called him, grew into a wonderful, loving dog that had one speed—barely medium. Day after day I would play chase recall games, throw tennis balls, spit liver at him as a reward, yet nothing increased his speed. No matter what tricks I pulled out of my hat, Tang never went faster than a trot. He trotted in on a recall. He trotted in and out on retrieves. He trotted while the rest of the dogs raced around the yard like wild banshees. Trotting was Tang's speed. It drove me nuts. Finally, when I could stand it no more, my husband, Rolf, took over Tang's training. He diligently and patiently trained Tang and put a Companion Dog Excellent (CDX) title on him. Tang's speed limitations never bothered Rolf.

On the other hand, my Border Collie, Rio, was a fast-moving dog from the time he was a baby. He is busy, crazy, active, and wild about working and training. That's luck. In the hands of an inexperienced handler Rio would be completely out of control, but he would still be fast.

Find Me

As previously mentioned, the "find me" game is used to build a strong play/prey drive. It's really nothing more than a modified hide-and-seek game, but it's a great way to foster the bond between you and your puppy. Additionally, it begins conditioning your puppy that you are his primary source of fun. It's also the preliminary stages of teaching the "recall" or "come" exercise. You teach your puppy (in a fun and exciting manner) to always find you when you say his name. You can play indoors or outdoors. (If you play the game outside, be sure to stay in an enclosed area so that your puppy cannot escape.)

You can run from one room to another. Hide behind a chair or a door, or even under a bed. Call your puppy's name enthusiastically. "Puppy! Puppy! Puppy!" When he finds you, praise him lavishly. Tell him he is brilliant and clever. Sit on the floor and shower him with hugs and kisses. If you are outdoors, duck behind a tree, a rock, a bush, a parked car, or a building—whatever is convenient—and say your puppy's name in a happy, enthusiastic tone of voice. When he finds you, again shower him with tons of praise. Any time I say my puppy's name, I want him to think, "That wild person is calling me again and something wonderful is involved!"

A variation on this game is to have someone hold your puppy at one end of the house as you run to the other end saying your puppy's name enthusiastically. Tell the person to release the puppy and give him the command "Find mom," or "Find him." You want to build enthusiasm, foster your puppy's zany personality and build an intense eagerness and unwavering desire for him to be with you. I play a lot of hide-and-seek and chase recall games with my puppies. It helps them to grow into adults that are willing to climb over, crawl under, or go through anything to get to me.

Find It

"Find it" is a similar game. Rather than teaching your puppy to find you, you teach him to find an object. This helps to build a strong retrieve drive. It also helps the puppy learn to use his nose, which is valuable for future scent discrimination or tracking. For instance, you hide a tasty tidbit of food, such as a piece of boiled liver, under a bucket or in a box. Encourage your

Building speed in a puppy will train him to do fast retrieves as an adult. Photo © Judith Strom.

puppy to use his nose to "find it." Toss a tidbit of food or his favorite toy down the hallway and encourage him to "find it." In the beginning, you might have to run with him to encourage or help him. When he finds the toy or food, tell him he is a super boy! Pump up his ego by letting him strut around and savor his clearly mammoth achievement.

Always play these games when you are sure he will succeed. If you call your puppy when he is playing with other puppies or eating his dinner, the chances are he will be too distracted and will not respond to your command. Any time this happens you have inadvertently set your puppy up to ignore you. Always set your puppy up to succeed rather than fail.

Always set your puppy up to succeed.

An eleven-week-old puppy learns to do a "twist."

Twist and Spin

Teaching a puppy to "twist" is a simple, fun command that helps to increase his vocabulary and stimulate his mind. It is guaranteed to impress and amaze your family and friends. Start with a tasty morsel of food in your right hand. Hold it close to your puppy's nose and simply guide him in a counter-clockwise circle. When he completes the circle, tell him "Good twist!" and reward him with the morsel of food. It's that simple. Eventually, the goal is to get him to "twist" on command without the food being used as a lure. This is accomplished through repetition and consistency—just as with any other exercise or command.

The "spin" is the same game, except rather than counter-clockwise, the puppy "spins" clockwise. When he has completed the circle or "spin," reward him with a tasty tidbit and verbal praise.

Both the twist and the spin are excellent games to transition from one exercise to another without breaking the excitement and momentum. For instance, you can play, play, play, and then do a "sit," praise, "spin," praise, "walk-back," praise, "down," praise, "sit," praise. Finish by throwing a toy behind your puppy as you tell him "Get it."

Walk-Back

Teaching the walk-back is a bit more challenging but equally impressive once mastered. Teach this exercise with the puppy on leash so you can maintain control. Again, start with a tasty tidbit of food. Use your index finger and thumb of both hands to hold the food about knee high. Bend your knees so you make a small chute. With your puppy standing and facing you, have him sniff or nibble the tidbit of food. As he does so, take small steps toward him that will cause him to move backwards. When he takes a step backward, tell him "Good walk-back!" or "Look at you!" The goal is for him to walk backward on command without assistance.

Most puppies possess a natural tendency to bite their leash. Rather than scold him, use the behavior to teach the

Use a tidbit of food to lure your puppy in front of you as you hold the food about knee height. Let him sniff the tidbit. Photos © Lana Young Photography.

Using the food to keep the puppy in position, step towards him and encourage him to take a step backward. Praise him, "Good walk-back!"

walk-back. Start by creating some resistance. Encourage the puppy to tug on his leash. Simultaneously create additional resistance by applying pressure at your end of the leash. At this point, the situation should resemble a bit of a tug-of-war. To get your puppy to walk-back simply take one step toward him. The sudden lack of resistance automatically will cause your puppy to take one or two steps backward. As he walks backward, praise him with "Good walk-back."

When your puppy has mastered the command, the "walk-back" becomes a premium game to transition from one exercise to another without creating a lull or break in the excitement. Again,

play with your puppy. Tell him "walk-back," and praise him. Do a "sit," then praise him. Continue with "Walk-back," praise, "down," praise, "sit" praise, "spin," praise, "walk-back," and so forth. Keep the momentum and excitement high by mixing up the commands.

TEACHING THE WALK-BACK.
Step one: *Let your puppy tug on his leash, thereby creating resistance.*

Step two: *Maintain the resistance for a few seconds by pulling on the leash as your puppy continues to tug.*

Step three: *Release the tension on the leash by stepping into your puppy. The sudden lack of resistance will cause your puppy to automatically walk backwards. Praise with "Good walk-back."*

INSTILLING ATTENTION AND FOCUS

The next few games will build attention and focus. Let me clarify that, in my opinion, "attention" differs from "focus" despite the fact that handlers often use them interchangeably. Depending upon your chosen field of competition, there can be a significant difference in their meaning. To me, focus is when a puppy or adult dog is focusing on a specific task at hand—like paying attention to where he is in heel position or straight fronts, retrieving an item properly, or maneuvering a dog walk correctly. He is focused on the task his handler is asking him to perform.

Attention is the foundation for a good performance. If you do not have your puppy's attention, you cannot teach him anything. Attention is a learned behavior. In obedience, it is learning to ignore distractions (other people, dogs, noises, smells) while maintaining a specific head position, such as in heel position. "Taught" or "forced" attention is very different from "voluntary" attention. In obedience, "taught" attention is demanding a specific head position and eventually correcting the dog for looking away. This technique creates a great deal of stress for the dog. He has to think more about where he is looking than about what he is doing. He is "watching" or paying attention because he does not want to be corrected. This type of forced attention affects the dog's overall attitude, and his performance usually suffers as a result.

Voluntary attention is motivated by using positive reinforcement. The dog is motivated to pay attention because it is fun to do so and there is a fantastic reward at the end—be it verbal or physical praise, play, or a tasty tidbit of food. This dog maintains head-position attention out of desire, rather than stress. He understands his job and has a positive mental attitude. As a result, he can maintain the attention effortlessly.

Many canine events, such as herding, require the dog to maintain a different type of attention. He is required to listen to and comply with his owner's commands while working or training. This form of attention differs from the learned head-position attention required in obedience. It would be impossible for a herding dog to do his job if he had to constantly maintain a specific head position.

Obedience handlers can put incredible stress on a dog by insisting on constant attention. Demanding that a dog constantly watch you when there's no real work going on between the two of you is boring to the dog. As a result, the dog often learns to give head-position attention, but he lacks mental attention—like the old adage "The lights are on but nobody's home." I have seen fantastic puppies grow up to work like robots because their handler drilled "attention" incessantly. Eventually there is not one shred of enthusiasm or desire left. The dog does his job because he has to, not because he wants to. There is a tremendous difference between an attitude that says, "What must I do today?" and one that screams "What are we going to do today?"

USING GAMES TO INCREASE FOCUS

Puppies are naturally curious. They are bursting with energy, excited about being alive, and eager to explore their new surroundings and collective aromas. Developing an adult dog that is happy, eager and motivated requires that you teach the puppy to focus on you rather than the myriad of surrounding sights and smells. Remember, fun creates focus. Focus maximizes a puppy's propensity to learn. The more your puppy focuses on you, the more you are able to teach him. The way I increase a puppy's focus on me is through interactive play.

> *Fun creates focus. Focus maximizes a puppy's propensity to learn. The more your puppy focuses on you, the more you can teach him. One of the best ways to increase a puppy's focus is to use interactive play.*

When I am training and playing with my puppy I like to keep moving. I will take a few steps forward, backward, or sideways while I talk to the puppy in an exciting tone of voice. Other times I will stand still and whisper. I try to see how low I can get my voice while still keeping my puppy's interest and curiosity. Sometimes I talk in an exciting, high-pitched voice or make funny noises. My puppy does not necessarily understand the words, but he

does understand the tone of my voice. Building a rapport with the puppy helps to maintain his focus and will ultimately help to reduce the stress of training and campaigning.

While I am carrying on a conversation with my puppy, I interject a few fun play-pops with his leash. I might wiggle my body or hop from side to side. I might do a 360-degree turn in front of him and then ask him in a happy voice, "Where did you go?" Occasionally I will turn my back on the puppy so he has to run in front to see my face. I ask him, "Where were you?" or "There's my silly boy!" If he does not run around to the front, I might bend over and peek at him between my legs. "I see you! You silly boy!" My spontaneity and enthusiasm keep the puppy's interest and focus on me.

If my puppy is very distracted with his surroundings I might get on the ground. I will begin picking inquisitively at the grass and asking no one in particular, "Ohhhh, what is that?" Most of the time a puppy's natural curiosity will get the best of him and he will rush over to explore the situation. Like the neighborhood busybody, he will need to know exactly what I am doing. When he starts poking his nose in the grass to see what I am up to, I will kiss his nose and say, "I got you!" I might touch his toes or toss some grass in the air. Never try to grab or restrain the puppy at this time. That would cause him to shy away, and in the future he will think twice about coming.

Tug-of-War

Tugging on the leash is a technique championed by Sylvia Bishop. I integrated this game into my training about twelve years ago and have had tremendous success. I know, for years you have worked diligently to keep your puppy from jumping and tugging at his leash and now I am telling you to encourage that behavior! I do this for a couple of reasons. First, I do not always have a

An eleven-week-old puppy learns to tug on his leash.

A sixteen-week-old puppy masters the game of tugging on his leash.

cookie or toy in my back pocket, but I always have my puppy's leash with me. In training, I let him tug, tug, tug. While he is diligently tugging away, I gently release the pressure so he quickly folds into a down. "Look at you! You're doing a down!" I let him continue tugging for ten seconds and then gently pop him into a sit. "Look at you! Aren't you clever," I will tell him. Sometimes I gently bounce the puppy back and forth. As he is tugging on the leash I pivot into heel position and take one or two steps. Or, while he is tugging and playing, I might pop my puppy between my legs, spin around, play some more and repeat one of the above exercises. Alternately, I will move on to another game without losing the puppy's focus. Do anything to *keep it fun!*

Furthermore, if I teach my puppy to play with his leash when he is a baby, when he is an adult dog in a competitive environment, I can wind him up on the way to the ring by engaging in a game of tug with his leash. When we finish competing, I can release any po-

tential anxiety by engaging in a game of tug or letting him shake and "kill" his leash as we run back to the exercise pen.

I bet you are thinking, how will my puppy be able to differentiate between playing and working? You certainly do not want your conformation or obedience dog to arbitrarily jump up and start tugging on his leash during a crucial judging time. Therefore, teach him a trigger word, such as "get it" or "kill it" or "tug." A Sylvia Bishop trick is to double the leash over so he quickly learns that when the leash is doubled over, he can tug on it. When the leash is not doubled over, he is to leave it alone. It is also beneficial if you teach him a release word, such as "give" or "out" or "drop it." This helps you to remain in control of the situation. If you cannot get the puppy to release the leash on command when playing, he is well on his way to taking full control. You have inadvertently relinquished your control and position as top dog. Besides, if he will not release the leash, how can you continue to play interactively?

TO TRAINING ALONE

Try some of these creative tips to stay focused, keep on track, and maintain enthusiasm when training alone.

1. Set a goal every time you go out to train. For a puppy it can be as simple as speeding up a slow recall, teaching a new exercise, or playing a fun game.

2. Create your own distractions. Tell your puppy to "watch" and then drop a ball or toy next to him. Leave toys or tidbit of food scattered around the training building or yard as you train. Train with the radio or television on for added distractions.

3. Work on the hardest or most stressful exercises first before your puppy gets tired.

4. Practice heeling *without* your dog. Try walking in a straight line or doing about turns while shopping at the grocery store, walking to the bus stop, or waiting for the dentist.

5. Be consistent in your training. A puppy cannot find "heel" or "front" if those positions shift.

6. Always look at your puppy when you are praising. Make sure he knows you are talking to him.

7. Keep the gray areas out of your training. Tell your puppy exactly what you are doing. If you are heeling and you drop your puppy's toy, don't just stop and pick it up. Release him. Tell him what you are doing, "Ooops! I dropped your toy!" Then pick up the toy. Play for a few seconds and then start heeling again.

8. Learn to be objective about what your puppy is or is not doing. Ignoring a situation is not an acceptable remedy if you want to be a successful handler or trainer.

9. Read books, watch training tapes, and attend as many training seminars as possible. There is always room for improvement.

10. The key to becoming a successful handler is to believe in yourself and your dog.

Cookie Toss Game

Most puppies possess a strong food drive and a natural desire to chase down food. That's why this game is so effective. I play this game with all my puppies, regardless of their age, because it's easy and fun and it builds excitement and focus quickly. If your puppy has a tendency to run off, you can play this game on a Flexi or longline. I start with a handful of tasty tidbits of food. Any type of scrumptious food that has some density (such as leftover steak, chicken, cheese, tortellini) will work. Crunchy dog bones or kibbles are less effective. The goal is to build speed, enthusiasm and focus, not to have your puppy spend ten or fifteen seconds crunching a hard biscuit. Remember, train with those $100 bills. The pieces of food should be big enough for your puppy to see at a good distance. They should be solid in composition so they do not break when they hit the floor.

I stand in the middle of my training building to play this game. You can also play this game in your living room or on the driveway. Playing on grass is not as productive because the puppy cannot find the cookie as quickly and you lose the momentum of the game.

Show the puppy a tasty morsel of food. Toss the food six or seven feet ahead of the puppy across the floor. Encourage him to "get it." Ninety-nine percent of the time puppies will tear across the floor and pounce on the food (especially if you are using food that is mouth-watering and irresistible to them.) As the puppy finishes scarfing down the food, say his name, "Fido." When he looks at you, show him a second piece of food and say, "Hurry, hurry, hurry!" As he runs toward you, toss the piece of food six or seven feet toward the other side of the room. This causes the puppy to run past you as he charges to get the food.

When he picks up the food, repeat the entire process again. Say his name, "Fido," and when he looks, say "Hurry,

hurry, hurry!" to build excitement. When he gets the tidbit of food and starts toward you, let him see you toss another piece of food in the opposite direction. Keeping yourself in the middle of the action helps to establish you as the center of the activity.

Once the puppy is charging enthusiastically back and forth across the building for tidbits of food, begin incorporating other fun behaviors. For example, as he comes charging back, toss a tidbit of food through your legs. Encourage him to run through your legs to get the treat. As he charges through your legs, you might spin around, face him and lure him into a "sit," "down," or "front." If he thoroughly understands the command, tell him to sit, down or front rather than luring him with a treat.

If your puppy sits crooked, do not fuss and fidget trying to fix it. Do not deflate his ego by nagging him. Let it go. At this point you want to *praise the effort and continue building focus and excitement.* However, be prepared the next time by having a clear and concise picture of the behavior you want to create. Strive to create it without nagging or fussing with your puppy. With a little imagination you can create variations of the game in order to instill specific behaviors in a fun and exciting manner while continuing to generate focus.

Watch Game

My Border Collie, Bronco, loves this game so much that he will virtually force his body between my legs and beg me to play it with him. When he is in the house with me, he will go around the house randomly picking up objects and bringing them back to me, trying to entice me to play the Watch game. The object of the game is to motivate head position and attention by making it into a game.

Step one: Put your puppy in a "sit" and straddle him so your legs are snug against his body. Put your fingers in his buckle collar under his chin and use your fingertips to tilt and gently hold his chin and head upward. This should leave your thumbs free to stroke and caress the bridge of his nose. At this point, his head position should be such that he has no choice but to be watching you. When you get the head position and eye contact, tell him "Good watch!" or "Watch."

I like to talk about a reward when I am working on attention. For example, when my puppy is watching me, rather than constantly bore him to death with "Watch," I say, "I've got a cookie!" or "Want to play?" I will tuck his toy under my chin and then tap it as I say, "Where's your ball? Do you want it?" The goal is twofold. First, you want to make "watch" a fun game. Second, you want to gradually increase the length of time your puppy maintains head and eye position. Remember, you are working with a very young puppy—often eight or ten weeks old. Getting from point A to point D will take more than a few days. Depending on your puppy, it could take months.

Step two: Go to this step when your puppy is more mature and can maintain his head position and eye contact without you continually holding his head.

Get your puppy into position and watching you. Then toss a favorite toy or a tidbit of food on the floor a few inches in front of the puppy. At first, your puppy will naturally be inquisitive and want to look at the tossed item. In some cases, he will even try to snatch it up off the ground. Remember, the object of the game is to maintain his head and eye position while paying attention to you rather than the tidbit of food or toy. If his head moves in the direction of the tossed object, simply use your fingers to quickly reposition it in the "watch" or "attention" position. When you have reestablished eye contact, remind him in a pleasant voice, "That's your watch," or simply "watch." The

An adult dog demonstrates the goal of the "watch game." Downward pressure is added to the bridge of his nose. If taught correctly, the dog will resist any downward pressure, thereby making "watch" a game.

The reward for "watching" is getting his dumbbell, toy or food on the ground in front of him.

command "watch" comes after you have repositioned his head and reestablished eye contact—not during the repositioning.

The reward for watching you is the toy or tidbit of food. In the beginning, when your puppy has maintained his head position (i.e., watching you) for five or ten seconds, gently wrap your hands around his muzzle, point his nose in the position of the food and tell him

"Look." Then give the command "Get it" or "Take it."

The goal is to gradually increase the amount of time he maintains his head position. Do not stretch the time so far that you end up losing his attention. It's important to progress at a rate that is suitable for the age and mental development of your puppy.

Step three: As your puppy matures and begins to thoroughly understand the game, follow the above steps to get him into position. After you have established eye contact and head position, relax the upward pressure of your fingertips. Talk to him so you encourage head position and eye contact. Ask him, "Where's your ball?" or "What are we going to do?" Praise your puppy when he maintains eye contact and head position.

To teach the "watch game" utilizing the leash, straddle your puppy. As he tugs on his leash, use resistance to hold his head in the "watch" position. Use your voice to get eye contact. When head and eye position are achieved, praise him for a "Good watch!"

When the puppy has maintained head and eye position for a few seconds, bounce him out in front of you and continue to encourage him to tug on his leash.

"Aren't you clever!" or "Good watching!" Release, play, and repeat three or four times in succession.

If, when you release the upward pressure, your puppy's head or eyes move downward, re-position his head with your fingertips and remind him in a pleasant voice, "That's your watch." (Always use your fingertips. Never bang or slap your puppy under his chin with your hand.) With his head in the desired position, toss his toy or food on the floor a foot or so in front of him. Remind him to "watch." Release. Play. Repeat.

Step four: Many more months down the line, when my puppy has mastered the above game, I begin adding downward pressure to the bridge of his nose with my fingertips. Timing on this exercise is critical. A split second after I apply downward pressure to the bridge of his nose, I apply upward pressure under his chin with the fingertips of the opposite hand. Simultaneously, I remind him to "watch." Eventually, if done correctly, your puppy will begin resisting the downward pressure. The more pressure you apply, the harder he will attempt to hold his head in the correct "watch" position.

While you should definitely strive to make this a fun game, it is a static

Remember: puppies learn at different rates. Never progress at a speed faster than your puppy's ability to comprehend.

A Word of Caution:

The "watch" command (or any other words you use at this time) should always be positive. If you get upset and jerk your puppy's head into position and tell him in an angry voice, "WATCH ME!", then watch becomes very negative. Similarly, if your puppy is "watching," but sees a snarling face glaring back at him, guess what your puppy is not going to want to do? (Some trainers like to use the word "ready" rather than "watch" because in an obedience competition the last thing the judge asks you before beginning an exercise is "Are you ready?" When the handler replies "Ready" it is an additional cue for the dog to pay attention.)

Place your fingers in his collar with your fingertips pointing upward to maintain his head position. Tuck a ball under your chin, and use your voice to encourage eye contact. Then drop the ball from your chin and encourage your puppy to catch it.

exercise and the puppy can quickly become bored or stressed. Therefore, do only three or four repetitions at a time. Be sure to keep the play exciting and rewarding after each repetition.

The Leash Tug

A variation on the above game is to straddle your puppy as you encourage him to tug on his leash. Use the resistance on the leash to maintain his head position. Your verbal praise, "Look at you!" will help to develop eye contact. Once your puppy has maintained head and eye position for several seconds, bounce him forward between your legs as you encourage him to continue tugging on his leash.

As your puppy begins to mature, place your fingers in his collar under his chin (fingertips pointing upward) and tuck a ball under your chin. Use your hands to maintain head position while utilizing your voice to maintain eye contact. Tell him he is clever. "Look at you! Are you watching your mom?" When he has maintained eye contact for a few seconds, drop the ball from your chin and let the puppy catch it. Have a quick game of tug before repeating the exercise.

Collar Pops

In the past, training methods have generally utilized collar pops as a form of correction. Therefore, the collar pop always had a negative association. I turn it around and make collar pops a fun, positive game. Hence, in training I can play pop my puppy's collar to motivate and stimulate him rather than correct him. As he grows and matures, I can use play pops in a competitive environment to rev him up and subsequently generate excitement. It is instructive to reiterate that the play collar pops are not corrections. You should be play popping your puppy's collar as you tell him, "Atta boy!" or "Look at you!" or "Good boy!"

I start by teaching my puppy right away that my hand in his collar or playful collar pops with his leash are fun games. I never want my puppy to think that my hand in his collar means he is bad or that something awful is going to happen. If I am sitting on the floor playing with my puppy, I slip one or both hands in his collar and continue playing. Other times while I am sitting on the floor playing I will gently push him away and then quickly pop him forward with his leash and collar. I tell him in an exciting voice, "I got you! You silly boy." Or I ask him, "Ohhh, what was that?" Again, my puppy does not necessarily understand the words but he will recognize my animated and delightful tone of voice. If I am in my training building or outside on the lawn working with my puppy, I randomly incorporate fun and playful collar pops into our playing and training. The key is that they must be quick and they must be executed in a positive and favorable attitude. Remember: You are gently popping and releasing the collar, not tugging on it.

Collar POPS are fun, not corrections!

Control Game

This game is best played on leash. The goal is to teach your puppy both focus and control, as well as quick responses to your commands. Everything you do in obedience training should have a purpose.

For this exercise, think ahead and imagine how this game will create fast and reliable sits on the go-out exercise. First, wind your puppy up by playing with him for a minute or two, then take off running. Run six or eight feet, then stop suddenly, step into your puppy and give a light but quick upward play pop on the lead so your puppy sits. Tell him, "Good sit!" or "Look at you!" Have him hold his "sit" for a few seconds then release him and immediately start playing with him again. Repeat this exercise several times in succession. Perform the entire activity with extreme excitement. There should not be a lull or break between the playing and the sitting. If you keep the game fast paced and exciting you will keep your puppy's focus on you and eventually develop fast sits.

This is the only time I advocate collar pops with a very young puppy. The collar pops are fun, playful pops, not corrections! This is a critical point. Give the collar pops in a brisk, positive, and stimulating manner so the puppy interprets them not as a correction but as a fun game.

As your puppy grows and matures and begins to build his vocabulary of commands, you can play this game utilizing various commands. For instance, follow the same steps as above but substitute a "down" or "stand" for the "sit" command. Try to project ahead in your training. Visualize how this game will help to instill a fast and reliable "down" for agility or herding, or an impressive "drop" on the drop-on-recall exercise.

DENVER, THE CHRONIC SNIFFER

Denver was eleven weeks old when I brought him home. Like all English Cockers, he was charming and irresistible, and he lived to sniff the ground. His life revolved around sniffing. This presents a unique training challenge when you compete in canine events such as obedience or conformation that require the dog to work with his head up.

With Denver, as well as all of my English Cockers, I consistently discouraged sniffing in a training situation. From the day he arrived at my home, I never allowed him to pick up food off the floor while we were training. I kept his leash short but not tight. If I dropped a tidbit of food and he tried to grab it, the leash prevented him from doing so. When he looked back at me I rewarded him with a tidbit and plenty of praise: "Look at you!" or "Good boy!"

I also kept food in my mouth and both of my hands. When I rewarded him with food, he never knew where it was going to come from. It might come from my left hand and then my right hand, or it might come from my mouth and then my left hand. Another time it might come from both of my hands simultaneously. This kept him excited and interested.

I used a lot of play and fun games to motivate him to hold his head upward. I played tug games with his leash, encouraging him to hold his head up by gently tugging upward. I hid toys under my arms and chin and asked him, "Where's your toy?" This kept his focus on me, not the ground. I always released the toy as he was looking upward.

Through association, repetition and consistency, Denver learned the picture and routine. He quickly learned that the only way he was going to get food or toys was by looking at me. Therefore, his head would automatically come up every time he was in heel position. I never had a problem with him sniffing in the obedience ring. When I released him from a training situation his head would immediately go down to the ground, and he would continue to sniff until the next training situation. I did not care if he sniffed when we weren't training and never discouraged sniffing outside of a training situation. It is unrealistic to expect a dog to never sniff.

These techniques helped Denver to excel in both obedience and conformation. He retired with a Companion Dog title as well as AKC and CKC Championships and multiple group wins.

Bobbie Anderson going High in Trial with one of her English Cockers, AKC & CKC Ch. Ceridwen Steel Bonnet UDX, "Raider."

Block Eight:
Teach Basic Skills

WHETHER YOUR GOAL IS OBEDIENCE, herding, agility, conformation, lure coursing, Schutzhund or any of the myriad of canine activities available—your puppy must learn some elementary obedience skills. My techniques will undoubtedly vary from other trainers. The bottom line, however, remains the same: to produce an adult dog that responds quickly, enthusiastically, and reliably to any command. My dogs compete in herding, obedience, tracking and conformation, yet my method for teaching the basics remains fundamentally the same. I teach chase recalls, folding downs, and tuck sits to all of my dogs. I try to remain open to altering, customizing, or tweaking a technique to accommodate the puppy's individual personality, temperament and mental capability.

Most trainers who train dogs specifically for stock work or herding trials tend to be less concerned with style, precision and detail than trainers who compete in obedience. The reason that I teach the "folding down" is because it prevents any forward motion on the obedience drop-on-recall exercise. A stock dog trainer, however, is not going to be as particular about style or precision. Likewise, when an agility

trainer asks for a sit, they are not concerned with whether or not the dog sits straight.

Regardless of the method you utilize, the puppy should mature into an adult dog that responds reliably and quickly to any given command. My Border Collies can go from a herding trial to an obedience ring without missing a beat. If one of them is ten feet away in the obedience ring and I tell him "Down," he downs without hesitation. If the same dog is working sheep 100 yards away from me and I tell him "Lie down," he hits the deck immediately. Down means down—regardless of the situation. The point is, the specific method (i.e., folding down versus a traditional down) is not as important as getting a quick and reliable response.

INSTILLING QUICK
AND CONSISTENT RESPONSES

You develop quick and consistent responses to commands by teaching a puppy while he is within a two- or three-foot radius of you. When your puppy thoroughly understands a command and is responding reliably while he is near you, then you can gradually begin adding distractions and distance. If you can't get a dog to respond quickly and reliably to a "down" command when he is two feet away from you, what is your game plan when he is 100 yards away and focused on stock?

As I mentioned in the Introduction, there are many wonderful methods for training puppies. My goal is to offer you some additional techniques that will help you to build a solid foundation and trusting relationship with your puppy, and also help to instill enthusiasm, motivation, and an unwavering desire to work.

Let me add that the behaviors you teach in a training environment will be the behaviors you get in a competitive environment. If you accept slow downs in a training situation, you will get slow downs in a competition. If you tell your puppy "Down" six times before he is required to respond, then you will get the same lack of response from your dog in a competitive situation. A puppy that learns to respond to a command slowly and in his own good time will not magically grow into an adult dog that performs quickly and enthusiastically. On the other hand, if a puppy learns from day one that "down" means hit the deck fast and do it on the first command, he will carry that attitude into a competitive environment.

> The behaviors you teach in a training environment will become the behaviors you get in competition.

TEACHING ELEMENTARY OBEDIENCE SKILLS

That said, let me explain the basic commands that I teach and my personal method for teaching each of them.

The Tuck Sit

There are several ways to teach the "sit" command. Personally, I teach the tuck sit—especially for competitive situations—because the puppy learns to quickly tuck his rear tightly under his body rather than rocking back into a sit. This looks much sharper in the ring because you get a fast, tight sit. Let me hurry to add (again) that I never use a collar pop when I am teaching the sit. Many methods advocate this policy, but I firmly believe that a puppy should get collar pops only in play.

This technique is quite simple and easy enough for even the greenest handler. Start with the puppy on leash. This way, you are always in control of the situation, especially if your puppy has his own agenda or tends to wander off or, like most puppies, is easily distracted. Hold the leash and a tasty tidbit of food in your right hand. Hold the food between your thumb and index finger. Keep your left hand free so when it comes time to tuck your puppy's rear, you will be ready. Start by playing with the puppy for a minute or two. Get him excited about being with you. Lure the puppy across the front of your body and raise the cookie in a slightly upward and backward direction directly above his nose. Simultaneously use your left hand to tuck his rear into a sit. Praise him with "Good sit," and then reward him with food. Release and play with him. Repeat the exercise three or four times in a row.

With a very young puppy, seven or eight weeks old, I like to get on the floor and play a tug game. Then I gently pop the puppy into a sit (as briefly illustrated earlier). To reiterate, I will play, tug, play, tug. As the puppy is tugging, tugging, tugging, I gently pop him into a sit. "Good sit!" Or I might do a spin as he is tugging on the toy, and then use the toy to gently guide him into a sit as he comes out of the spin. This helps to develop a fast response to the sit command.

To teach the tuck sit, kneel on the ground close to your puppy. Hold the leash and a tidbit of food in your right hand between your thumb and index finger. Lure the puppy across the front of your body, keeping the food close to his mouth.

Raise the food upward and backward as you tuck the puppy's rear into a sit. Praise, and reward with food.

Step one: Start with your puppy in a stand. Put your left hand in his collar as illustrated, and show him a tasty tidbit of food.

Step two: Simultaneously apply backward and downward pressure on the collar as you move the food in a downward motion between his front feet. Praise and reward him with food.

The Folding Down

I teach the "folding down" because it teaches the puppy to plant his front feet and then fold his body backward into a down. Not only does this technique look nice, it also helps to eliminate any forward motion in the drop-on-recall.

Start with a handful of tasty tidbits. (Use $100 bills—chicken, liver, or steak.) Kneel or sit on the floor so you are at eye level with him and therefore less intimidating. Start with the puppy standing. Let him know you have an inviting morsel of food in your hand. Place your hand in his collar with your fingertips pointing downward. Simultaneously move the food down between his front legs, toward the floor directly below his chest, and apply downward and backward pressure with the hand in his collar. Done correctly, this will cause the puppy to plant his front feet and fold his body into the down position. Praise him with "Good down," and reward him with the food. Repeat the command three or four times in a row, with two or three fun sessions throughout the day.

Every so often a young puppy, for whatever reason, will resist the hand in his collar. If you run into this situation, follow the above steps but, instead of putting your hand in his collar, apply light pressure on his shoulders.

Some puppies will have a difficult time grasping the concept of planting their feet and following the food into the down position. If you have this problem, try placing your thumbs in the hollow between the puppy's breastbone and shoulders and wrapping your fingers around his shoulder blades. Tell him "Down" while simultaneously pushing him in a gentle downward and backward movement into the down position. Praise him with "Good down!" Reward him with the tidbit, then release him with plenty of fuss and fanfare.

If you prefer, you can use your puppy's favorite ball or squeaky toy instead of food when teaching this exercise. Follow the same steps as above, substituting his favorite toy for the food. With all exercises, you should be able to use food and toy motivators interchangeably as your puppy matures.

If your puppy resists your hand in his collar or the downward pressure on the collar, follow the steps on the previous page but, rather than putting your hand in his collar, apply light pressure on his shoulders.

FOLDING DOWN USING A TOY.
Step one: *With your puppy in the standing position, place your hand in his collar as illustrated earlier.*

Step two: *Simultaneously apply backward and downward pressure on the collar as you move the toy downward between the puppy's front feet. When he is in the down position, reward with plenty of verbal praise and the toy.*

Teaching "Come" with Two People.
Step one: *Both people sit on the ground. One person holds the puppy while the second person simultaneously shows him a toy or a tidbit of food while saying his name enthusiastically, and then the "come" command.*

Step two: *The first person lets go of the puppy while the second person continues to call his name enthusiastically.*

The reward for coming is the tasty tidbit of food or his toy and plenty of praise. Photos © Lana Young Photography

Coming When Called

Coming when called is one of those rudimentary skills all puppies must learn. It is the cornerstone of future exercises. Since you are going to teach him to "come," you might as well teach him to "come" in a speedy, reliable, and enthusiastic manner. After all, who wants a puppy that nonchalantly saunters back when you can have a puppy that flies in at top speed?

In addition to being awe-inspiring, a reliable recall will free you and your dog to further enjoy the human/canine relationship. Instilling the behavior is not difficult provided you have not allowed your puppy to develop the bad habit of ignoring you.

First, from day one, never put a puppy in a position where he has the opportunity to run away or mingle with other puppies while he is being trained. If a puppy has a tendency to wander, immediately attach a lightweight longline to his buckle collar. If he starts to stray, you should simply step on the longline. As he stops and looks back to see what is going on, praise him for looking at you. When he starts back toward you, praise him, "Good job!" When he gets to you, praise him again and reward him with a cookie.

If you step on the longline and the puppy does not show the slightest intention of coming back, simply reel him in with the longline and shower him with plenty of praise. But do not give him a cookie. This same exercise can be used on an adult dog that has a tendency to wander or is interested in everything other than his owner.

One game that is fun to use to instill the "come" response in very young puppies is quite simple, but it does require at least two people. Both people sit on the floor facing each other, with their legs as wide apart as possible and the bottoms of their shoes touching. This forms a makeshift chute to guide the puppy. One person starts the game by holding the puppy while the second person shows the puppy a tidbit of food and enthusiastically calls the puppy's name. The person holding the puppy releases him. If all goes as planned, the puppy should run to the person who is calling his name. Keep the leash on the puppy and let it drag behind him as he runs from one person to the other. Greet the puppy with an abundance of hugs and kisses and a cookie. Tell him he is a "Clever boy!" or he is "Brilliant!" Kiss his nose and tell him he is irresistible. Repeat the exercise three or four times in succession. As your puppy progresses, begin increasing, and continue to gradually increase, the distance between the two people.

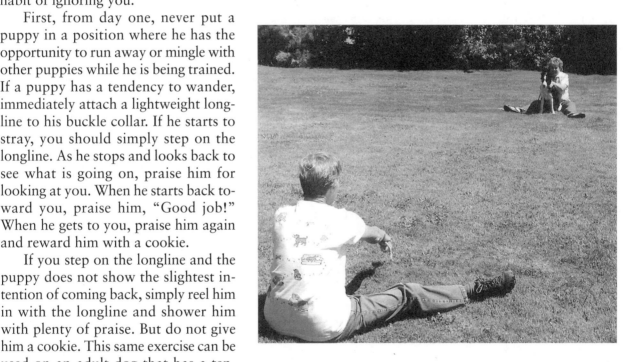

Increase the distance as the puppy learns and matures.

TEACHING THE CHASE RECALL.
Step one: *Ask someone to assist you by holding your puppy a few inches above the ground. Simultaneously, you show him a toy and ask, "Do you want it?"*

Step two: *While the assistant continues to hold the puppy, take off running, calling the puppy's name enthusiastically. When you are twenty-five feet or so away, your assistant lets the puppy go.*

Chase Recalls the Sylvia Bishop Way

Chase recall games are excellent motivators. This game, which is a variation of previously mentioned games, utilizes a form of resistance training as well as a puppy's natural chase instinct to teach a fast and enthusiastic recall.

Ideally, your puppy should be wearing a buckle collar—rather than a choke chain or prong collar—to prevent injury. Start by having someone hold your puppy by the leash. Hype your puppy up by showing him a tidbit of food or his favorite toy. I growl at my puppy—"Rrrrrrrrrrr"—or tap his chest or shoulder and ask, "Do you want to do recalls?" Telling the puppy what we are going to do (i.e., recall) helps to instill the name of the behavior in his mind and increase his motivation and drive. Then as he matures all I need to say is, "Do you want to do recalls?" and the dog goes wild because "recalls" have always been fun and exciting. This behavior will transfer to a competitive environment. In the obedience ring I can keep his attention on me as we move from one exercise to another. I ask him, "Do you want to do a recall?" This philosophy can be used with jumping, retrieving and so forth.

Once you've shown him the food or toy, take off running across the training building or yard as you enthusiastically say his name, "Fido! Fido! Fido!" Most puppies yip and lean into their collars because their natural instinct to chase is being incited. When you are halfway or so across the building or yard, the person holding your puppy lets him go. You should continue to encourage him with his name and his toy. The ultimate goal is for your puppy to tear across the room or yard with excitement and enthusiasm.

When the puppy gets to you, encourage him to run through your legs by throwing his favorite toy or a tidbit of food through your legs. Praise him lavishly. "Good come!" Then spin around, grab his toy and play with him for a few seconds before repeating the game.

A variation on this game is to follow the above steps, but, when the puppy starts toward you, turn your back on him and run another eight or ten feet away as you continue to encourage him. Stop and bend over, peek through your legs, and tell him, "Good one!" Get him to run through your legs. Reward him with the toy or food and plenty of genuine praise. Use your imagination and enthusiasm to create other fun and exciting recall games.

If your puppy is a bit reserved or cautious about playing, have the person holding your puppy slip their hands under his tummy and hold him two or three inches off the ground. Run across the room calling him enthusiastically while they hold him. Or they can stimulate him by asking, "Where's your mom?" Run across the room and get down on the floor with your arms and legs open to receive him as you call his name. By getting on the floor, eye level with your puppy, you are more inviting and less intimidating to him. When he gets to you, shower him with love and affection. Tell him he's adorable. If he is small enough, encourage him to climb up on you. Lavish him with praise and kisses.

The more you play this game and the more exciting you make it for your puppy, the more zealous your puppy will be about coming to you when called. The recall or "come" command will not be stressful because you have made it an amusing and fun game for the puppy.

If you do not have a partner to hold your puppy, there are several other ways to play the recall game. First, put your puppy on a longline or Flexi. As you are walking, let him get a little in front of you. Then suddenly back up and call your puppy enthusiastically. Tell him "Good come!" when he gets to you.

If you have access to a fenced yard, take your puppy for a walk and let him drag an eight- or ten-foot lightweight

Step three: As your puppy charges toward you, bend over, peek between your legs and say the puppy's name. Encourage him to run between your legs, then praise him for a "Good come!"

Step four: Pick up the puppy's leash and interact in a fun game of tug. Photos in this series © Lana Young Photography.

RESPECT IS THE KEY

When my Sheltie, Cajun, does not feel like working, I can say "Cajun, come!" and he will immediately turn and charge over to me with his head, ears, and tail up. He has never been allowed to think that "come" means to slowly or nonchalantly creep over to me at his own leisure. Nor has he been allowed to think that "come" means "Wait one second while I finish what I am doing." "Come" means come to me quickly, enthusiastically, and without hesitation, regardless of the situation. Again, the bottom line is respect. From day one, I instilled the behavior of respecting me.

line attached to his buckle collar. When he looks away, take off running in the opposite direction. Clap your hands and say his name enthusiastically. Usually the puppy's chase instinct will kick in and he will chase and catch up with you. Always reward the "come" behavior with a bounty of praise and plenty of tidbits.

TEACH IT RIGHT

Regardless of what exercise or command you are teaching, you must have a clear and concise picture in your mind of the behavior you are attempting to teach. If you cannot visualize it in your mind, how can your puppy achieve it? Therefore, first create in your mind the results you want in a competitive environment. Then work toward it in a training environment. This way, you will be able to create a clear vision for your puppy.

Suppose someone said to you, "Go to the corner and turn left—no, wait, turn right. Wait! Let me think about it. Okay, that's right. You go to the corner and turn left." You would be very confused. However, if they said, "Go to the first corner and turn left," you would

have no problem understanding the directions.

Help your puppy as much as possible by first creating in your own mind the performance you want in the ring and then work toward it. Practicing 100 crooked sits or 50 slow recalls will not teach your puppy to do it correctly. If you allowed him to sit crooked in training, why would you expect him to miraculously sit straight in the ring? It is better to do an exercise correctly one time than to do it incorrectly 100 times. Remember, you are not training for today—you're training for three years down the road when you will be competing. In the ring, you will not get a second chance to get it right. When training, do not fuss about the mistake and try to fix the problem after the fact. Instead, forget the goof-up and play with your dog to get him in the right frame of mind. Then set him up and help him to do it correctly the next time.

Always train for excellence. Teach with precision. This young Afghan is learning to follow hand movements for agility. Photo courtesy of Diane Bauman.

KEEP YOUR OPTIONS OPEN

One final piece of advice on training commands. Do not try to use the same training methods on all puppies regardless of their temperament. As I mentioned earlier, I like to have options in my training. Therefore, I make it a point to continually learn and accumulate an array of training methods. Think of your brain as an imaginary tack box stuffed full of training techniques. In the top drawer you could keep all the techniques and games you have accumulated on how to motivate your puppy. In the second drawer you could keep your trade secrets for building speed and enthusiasm. The third drawer is where you file away all the information you have accumulated for teaching basic obedience commands. You get the picture.

The point is, when you are training and you run into a problem, you should be able to dig into your imaginary tack box and pull out an alternative training method specific to your dog's personality and temperament.

KNOW WHEN TO

It is important to know when to stop training. If, for example, you are working on a retrieve and your puppy does two or three great retrieves, stop training retrieves for that session. Too often, handlers want to keep training and training. Eventually their puppy does the retrieve wrong because he is tired or bored. The handler then gets angry and cannot figure out what is wrong with their puppy's attitude.

If you get two or three good responses to a command, move on to another exercise. Do not keep hammering away at the same exercise.

USING DISTRACTIONS

Once your puppy has mastered a command in a non-distractive situation, you can begin incorporating mild distractions, such as a toy lying nearby on the floor. As he learns to pay attention and focus on you with mild distractions present, you can begin escalating the distractions. Have other trainers work their dogs nearby, train near other dogs running and playing, kick or drop a ball near your puppy. If your puppy has a difficult time focusing, perhaps the increase in distractions was too severe. Or possibly you need to increase the amount of excitement and energy you put out. Make yourself more exciting than the distractions. Eventually, your goal is for your dog to be able to focus on you in a competitive environment despite a myriad of distractions.

FORMAL VERSUS INFORMAL TRAINING

Try not to get caught up in the formal versus informal training philosophy. All the time people ask me, "When should I start my puppy in formal training?" The only real difference between formal and informal training is the degree of precision. You cannot draw a line in the sand and say, "Okay, this is formal training and that is informal training."

Few canine events require the precision of obedience. Therefore, if your goal is obedience titles (or multiple titles including obedience), then as your puppy matures you will need to ask for more and more precision. Formal training should never be all work and no play. It should be equally as fun as informal training. Again, the only difference is the degree of precision. You can build precision while still incorporating fun and games into your training. As you are playing and having fun, you should incorporate more formal body

language into your training sessions.

The goal is for your puppy to grow into a well-adjusted, happy adult that is eager and capable of executing a variety of commands under potentially stressful show conditions. Is that formal or informal training? Does it really matter?

What you absolutely want to avoid is "formal" training that is hideously boring for your puppy—the type of training that is repetitious and predictable. For example, if you are teaching your puppy how to "sit," rather than do eight boring sits in a row, try mixing up your routine. Get a toy and have a tug game. Then lure your puppy into a "sit," or, if he already knows the command, tell him to "Sit" rather than luring him. When he sits, praise him. Throw the toy behind him and encourage him to get it. When he picks it up, run across the building or yard and call him enthusiastically. Praise him for coming. Play with the toy some more. Then ask him to do a "spin" or a "twist," or push the toy into his front legs and watch him fold into a "down." Praise him, play some more, and then lure him into a "front". Praise him. Drop the toy behind you, open your legs and use your hands to gently push the puppy through them. Play some more, then throw the toy behind him as you both chase it.

Use your imagination to keep short training sessions fun and exciting. Use a lot of play so the puppy is always focusing on you and wanting to be with you. Become the most exciting aspect of his world. Always train for attitude and play for attitude.

Be creative with your training. Set your puppy up to do a recall; call him: "Come."

When your puppy gets the ball, tell him he is fantastic. Interact in a game of tug for a few seconds.

115

Keep the momentum going. While the puppy is tugging on the toy, pivot into heel position. Put your hands in the puppy's collar and bounce him two or three steps in heel position.

Let him hold on to the toy as you maneuver him into a sitting position. Ask him, "Are you doing silly heel work?"

PRACTICE VERSUS TRAINING

There is a significant difference between practice and training. Training is constantly striving to improve your puppy's performance, as well as your own. Practicing is running through the exercises to see how the training is progressing.

Always train the *parts* of an exercise and the behaviors, not the entire exercise. For example, if your junior herding dog is having trouble with his "down" command, remove him from the herding situation. Find the root of the problem, and then work on fixing the problem separately from the field work. Whatever you do, do not scream multiple commands at your dog. It does absolutely no good and it teaches him he does not need to respond immediately.

HOW OFTEN SHOULD YOU TRAIN?

I never train every exercise every day. That would be far too much for any puppy to comprehend. I do, however, train or expose my puppy to specific behaviors every day. When puppies are learning new behaviors, it is much easier for them to comprehend and progress through a behavior if you work with them every day. It's important, however, to avoid overworking your puppy. Never work him until he becomes either exhausted or bored and quits.

When I start a new puppy, I might do some fun recalls, a little name recognition, and then start on some "attention" work. I will play some fun retrieve games and perhaps finish the session by teaching the "sit" command. All of this takes about fifteen minutes. The following day I might do three or four fun "recall" games, a bit more "attention" work, a few fun retrieves, three or four "sits" and then start the "down" command. Again, all of this takes ten or fifteen minutes.

All training is done in a fun, exciting and informal atmosphere. I generally limit the training sessions to ten or fifteen minutes, one or two times a day. However, I continue to utilize every opportunity to instill a specific behavior when I am around the puppy in my daily routines. A cardinal rule of training is that you should consider every moment spent with your puppy as training. That's because every minute you spend with your puppy, you are instilling either desired or undesired behaviors.

For example, if I'm peeling carrots at the kitchen sink and my puppy is watching inquisitively, I ask him in a happy, exciting voice, "Are you watching your mom? What a good watch." I might lure him into a "sit" with a tiny piece of carrot and then praise him lavishly. "Good sit!" All of which took about thirty seconds.

If I am watching television. I might sit on the floor and rub the puppy's tummy and kiss his nose. I might put him in a "stand" and praise him, "Look at you! You're standing!" I might calmly rub my hands all over his tiny body, check his ears, rub his teeth, count his toes, or kiss his nose. Six months down the road he will not spook when a breed judge exams him.

When I take my puppy outside to potty, I utilize that opportunity as well to instill the "hurry, go pee" or "good pee" command. When he is finished, I race him back to the house. When he passes me and beats me to the door, I praise him. Again, it's being constantly aware of your puppy and taking advantage of every opportunity to cement the human/canine bond and instill mutual respect as well as specific behaviors. Training a puppy should be fun for *both* you and your puppy.

> **Train for attitude. Play for attitude!**

117

TEACHING THE STAND.
Step one: *Start with the puppy sitting. Place your hand in the collar, fingers pointing upward.*

Step two: *Hold the collar as you lift the puppy under his tummy, placing him in a stand. Praise him with "Good stand!"*

Block Nine: Build a Plan for Success

Setting goals is one of the most important, yet most neglected, aspects of any program. Goals force you to prioritize, provide incentive and motivation, build confidence, and provide a blueprint for success. It all starts with a plan.

People train and show dogs for a variety of reasons. For some it's an outlet for their competitive spirit. Some want to train or handle dogs professionally for the money, notoriety, or prestige. Some think their puppy is smarter or faster than anything else in the ring and want to show the world. Others simply want to broaden their puppy's horizons and have a little fun. Regardless of whether your objective is obedience, conformation, herding, Flyball, agility, Schutzhund, lure coursing, tracking, field work, or any other canine sport, defining your goals will maximize the probability of success.

REALITY CHECK— THE RIGHT PUPPY

It's important to be both honest and realistic in examining your motives before you set goals. If you are driven by the desire for big bucks, popularity, or the thought of making the rounds of national talk shows—keep in mind that a *very small* percentage of trainers and handlers reach celebrity status. That's not to say you cannot achieve enormous success both in and out of the competitive arena. Maybe you will even wind up with your own dog training show on cable television. Perhaps Lady Luck really is your best friend. Most top performance handlers, however, are just ordinary folk who juggle the demands of dog show travel and competition with family, personal, and social responsibilities, and even a part- or full-time job.

It is also very important that you are realistic and knowledgeable when evaluating the potential of your puppy. Almost any sound dog is capable of some level of successful performance competition. The dogs that are successfully competing at the top national or world levels, however, are talented individuals that have found their way into the hands of talented handlers.

My Border Collie, Ditto, is motivated and enthusiastic and he has a tremendous desire to please me. He loves to play with me, and he loves playing with other dogs. However, when I say, "Let's go train," he drops

If you want a future Schutzhund dog, it is wise to select one from a line of accomplished workers. This puppy is finding out what it is like to grip a bite sleeve. Photo © Judith Strom

Choose a puppy with the drive and personality to succeed in the performance event of your choice. This Shetland Sheepdog puppy is already carrying a tiny dumbbell. Photo courtesy Claudia Frank.

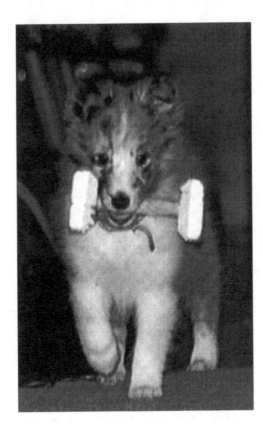

his head and slinks around with his tail between his legs. When he was younger, learning new tasks worried him tremendously because he did not like to make mistakes. Training was very stressful for him. But once he mastered a task, he was quite happy to comply.

My life would have been much easier had I chosen to sell Ditto or ship him back to the breeder. Instead, I had a goal that he would get his Obedience Trial Championship and be a top competitor in the obedience ring. He eventually did win multiple 200 scores in obedience, and even became a successful herding dog, because I set a goal and refused to give up. This, however, is an exception and not the rule. If you want to make it to the top, you are well advised to choose a puppy with the physical and mental fortitude, drive, and personality to succeed in the performance area that you choose.

The relationship between you and your puppy is a partnership tethered by an invisible umbilical cord. It should never matter what your best friend, another competitor, or even a judge thinks. The only thing that should matter to you is that you have a thorough understanding of what your puppy, as an individual, is capable of achieving.

A few years ago there was a young girl in my class that had gone to a dog show, watched the obedience dogs compete, and decided that was what she wanted to do. So she bought a Golden Retriever puppy and from that day forward, like a heat-seeking missile, she was locked on to what she thought she had to do in order to earn a 200 score. Day after day she attempted to train "ring routine," because that was the only "picture" of what she was working toward that she could visualize. Sadly, she never took into consideration her puppy's temperament and personality and what he, as an individual, was capable of achieving.

If you want a dog that is capable of a long and successful competitive career, there are are two major points to keep in mind.

First, when you are training a competition dog, you can't skip steps because, when you run into trouble, your puppy will not have a solid foundation of learning to fall back on.

Second, some people want a dog that is a compulsive worker (that's what the girl with the Golden wanted). If you don't have a naturally compulsive worker, you need to make him a compulsive worker before you start nitpicking the details required for a 200 score. Otherwise, you will burn him out.

Some puppies are born naturally compulsive workers. As these puppies grow and mature you can push them harder and demand more from them than from their counterparts. High-level achievement in performance events will be easier with this type of dog.

CRITERIA FOR GOALS

Setting goals is not difficult, but it does require certain criteria. Goals must be realistic. They must be specific. And they must be developed for both the long and short term. Finally, you must make a sincere commitment to your plan. Whatever goals you set, they must be your own—not someone else's. You and only you can decide what you want to achieve.

OUTCOME AND PERFORMANCE GOALS

Outcome goals usually involve comparisons with someone else, such as beating another handler or finishing number one in the country. The problem with outcome goals is that they are vulnerable to elements beyond your control, such as judges' decisions, weather, injuries, excellence in other

These terrier puppies are exploring the grounds at a working terrier trial. Will one of them be a future versatility champion? Photo © Judith Strom.

dogs and handlers, and just plain luck. Goals that are based solely on winning can set you up for failure.

Performance goals are based on personal targets or skills to be acquired. For example, you might set a goal of increasing your dog's speed, improving his speed or attitude over a previous performance, or developing a personal exercise program so you are physically fit and capable of keeping up with your dog. While you may, for whatever reason, fail to place in the ribbons, the compensation is that you can draw satisfaction and self-confidence from having reached a personal milestone.

Some experts suggest steering clear of outcome goals. There is, however, nothing wrong with wanting to finish number one in the country, or to win Best in Show or High in Trial, as long as the goal is kept in perspective. No one enters a show or trial and says, "Gee, I hope I lose today." Everyone wants to win, but you can get into trouble when you focus only on outcome goals and neglect performance goals. If you set an outcome goal, spend as much

Getting from point A to point D requires a plan. Photo courtesy Bobbie Anderson.

time, if not more time, focusing on your performance goals. In the end they will help you achieve your outcome goal.

LONG-TERM AND SHORT-TERM GOALS

To succeed, you will need to develop both long-term (yearly and career goals) and short-term goals (daily, weekly and monthly goals). A career goal might be designed to help you train and show the best dogs you can over the course of your lifetime. A long-term or yearly goal might be to successfully compete at a national or international competition or specialty. Short-term goals should be designed to bring you incrementally closer to your long-term goals. They keep you motivated and moving forward. Short-term goals should be realistic and exciting. They should be within your grasp if you really put the effort into them.

For example, sports psychologists often recommend that you start by identifying your long-term goal, such as competing at an international agility event. Once you have identified the goal, write the specifics on an index card: "June 24-26, Finland." Post the card on your tack box or refrigerator or someplace where you will see it often. Even when you are not consciously

reading the card, your mind will absorb it and eventually accept it as a mission.

To move step-by-step toward your long-term goal, you next set up specific short-term goals. Do you have to forgo some luxuries so you can afford to train with the best professionals or attend seminars? Do you have to undertake a serious fitness program that includes weight training so you can perform at your best? Do you need to schedule daily training and grooming time to ensure you work with your puppy regularly? Do you have to work within a budget to finance entry fees, travel expenses, and so forth?

I set goals but I don't set timelines. Every puppy/dog is different. It is dangerous to say, "This puppy must heel by the time he's sixteen months old." You can set a goal of having a dog ready for competition at two years, but write your goals into monthly, weekly, and even daily goals.

It's easy to say, "I am going to do A, B, C, and D with my puppy." However, getting from point A to point D is a step-by-step process that takes time and thought. You cannot skip steps. You cannot get from step A to step D without going through steps B and C. If you skip steps, your puppy's future performance will suffer because his foundation of learning will not be solid.

FINDING TIME TO TRAIN

by Joanne Carriera

Work, household tasks, and family time make the days fly, and all those good intentions to train your dog "every day" can get put on hold. But don't give up! With a little creative thinking, you can find the time for at least quick mini-sessions that add up to steady progress. Whether you want a well-behaved pet or have a competition dog, try some of our tips and tailor them to your own needs.

1. When you bring the kids to softball or soccer, bring your dog and work him at the edge of the spectator area. The result? You will have increased your dog's skill, trained him in a distracting area, and been an ambassador for responsible dog ownership.

2. When it's time to feed your dog, don't put his dish down just yet! Take a few tasty chunks from his bowl to use as rewards and put him through a few play-training exercises first. Then, when you do put down his dish, he will view it as a further reward for a job well done!

3. Watching your favorite TV show? Have your dog do a down during an act and a few recalls during the commercials.

4. Going for a walk? Do several paces of heeling off and on. Go "window shopping" and have him do a sit or down each time you stop.

5. Make a date with your dog! Mark a thirty-minute play and training appointment on your calendar and keep it!

6. Make a date with a dog-owning friend to practice together. It's a great way to motivate each other and socialize your dogs.

7. Keep obedience jumps or agility obstacles set up and pop your dog over them whenever you happen to go out in the yard.

8. Work on your dog's tracking skills while walking or going for your daily jog.

9. Practice long sits and downs while you are cooking or on the phone. Practice agility-type exercises on the playground equipment when you take your children to the park.

10. To prepare for those days when you can't train until after dark, scout out safe, well-lit parking lots, church yards and the like.

See how easy it is? You'll probably come up with more ideas of your own, too, and will be thrilled with your dog's progress!

Bobbie Anderson and her dog, OTCH Redtop Rio, UDX, going High In Trial. Competing successfully at such a high level is not a weekend game—it requires a full-time commitment.

PRIORITIES

If you want nothing more than to attend a few shows every year, put a performance title on a dog, and have a bit of fun, your goals will differ from those of someone who has dedicated their life to achieving excellence in the sport. Competing successfully at the top is not a weekend game; it is an every-day-of-the-year job. Your level of commitment is often the difference between success and failure.

For example, at a recent seminar, I heard a woman complaining endlessly about how she never had time for her dogs. "One of these days I am going to find time to train my dogs," she said with such conviction. The truth is, other things in this woman's life were more important than training her dogs. If you want to succeed on the top level, your dogs must become a priority. You must make the time for them on a daily basis. There is no wiggle room here. Make your puppy a priority. Make the time to train.

You can find a million reasons not to train: your job, kids to shuttle from school to soccer, bills to be paid, lawns to be mowed, and, of course, "Must see TV." More than a few of these steal away forever that short window of opportunity you have in which to shape your puppy's future.

Experts in time management often suggest charting or analyzing your day in fifteen- or thirty-minute increments. What type of pattern do you see: working, commuting, socializing, gardening, washing the car, surfing the Internet? Is puppy training in there anywhere? You will be surprised to see how easily an hour here and an hour there are wasted when you fail to manage your time. Can you dissect and reorganize your time more efficiently? No one will value your time quite like you do. Therefore, learn to manage it. When necessary, learn to say "No" and not feel guilty.

I train my dogs from 10:00 a.m. to noon. I never schedule doctor, dentist, or hair appointments or any other engagements between those hours. That's my time to train, and, barring an emergency, that is what I do during those hours, five to six days a week. It works for me. You need to find what works for you. Making the commitment is easy. The trick is to learn to control or schedule your daily life so that somewhere in a twenty-four-hour day you include some time for training your puppy.

MOTIVATING THE MOTIVATOR

You can set goals from now until doomsday, but unless you motivate yourself and find a way to continually sustain that motivation, your goals are destined to fall by the wayside. I mentioned in a previous chapter that the

Attending seminars is an excellent way to motivate yourself.

> **Obstacles are what you see when you take your eye off your goal.**

best way to motivate your puppy is to motivate yourself.

As stated earlier, people have different reasons for training dogs. For me, training dogs gives me pleasure—it's as simple as that. Some people love to golf or hike or race cars. I love to train dogs. That is when I am the happiest. As a young child I spent most of my time teaching the family dogs an assortment of amusing tricks. It was not until 1969, when I enrolled our ten-year-old daughter in a 4-H club, that I was introduced to "real" obedience. Six months later the 4-H instructor moved, so I bought a dog training book and took over the club. Life has never been the same.

Whatever your motivation, it must be genuine. Otherwise it's doubtful that you will succeed on a long-term basis. What motivates you will most certainly differ from what motivates other handlers and trainers. However, you can often gain increased motivation by watching top handlers training or showing. For instance, I find attending seminars extremely motivating. I always want to rush home and try the different training techniques, and figure out how to modify or tweak them to suit my puppy. It is exhilarating to watch an exceptional dog and handler team. They can take your breath away and make you yearn for that same kind of excellence.

SETBACKS—THE GRAND CANYON

Part of setting goals is learning to deal with the setbacks that inevitably occur. There will always be injuries, poor judging, inclement weather, people who disappoint you, and dips in your performance that can look like the Grand Canyon. The key to success is understanding that setbacks are endemic in the sport of dogs. Five steps forward, three steps back, and you are still two steps ahead.

The objective is to keep moving forward and not give up. It's okay to come up with an alternative strategy, or even revise your goals if necessary. Reassess, reevaluate, but do not panic. "Success is never final and failure is never fatal. It's courage that counts," wrote educator George Tilton. I cannot stress enough the significance of mustering the courage to take the necessary steps—and risks—to achieve your competitive goals.

There are talented handlers who simply have the wrong dog. There are also great dogs that are talented enough to overcome their handler's ineptitude. I would never advise a handler to quit on his or her dog. That is not my decision. It is important to focus on the positive aspects of your puppy and not dwell on the negative.

Start with the best puppy you can get, train diligently, set goals and stick to them, and, as a team, become the best that you can be.

Block Ten: Be Demanding

THE FOUNDATION OF YOUR TRAINING IS in place. Now you must make sure that no cracks appear, and that the blocks you built upon are firmly cemented together. No conversation on puppy training would be complete without talking about the importance of being demanding, as well as objective. Being demanding is not a bad quality. Although it probably is not a quality you desire in good friends or in-laws, it is a quality you must learn to cultivate if you are to succeed as a handler and trainer.

PAY ATTENTION TO DETAILS

If you want to win, you must pay attention to the little details. You cannot afford to ignore them. By being keenly attentive and focused on your puppy as he matures, you can immediately recognize and remedy problems before they become sizable stumbling blocks. Furthermore, you need to accomplish this with skill and finesse so as not to nitpick and crush your puppy's spirit.

At a show some months back my Border Collie, Rio, did a beautiful retrieve. However, when he sat in front I noticed that he chomped once on his dumbbell. The second day, he did another beautiful retrieve but when he sat in front it was chomp, chomp, chomp. Not one chomp but three! Some handlers would have been oblivious to the situation or possibly chosen to ignore it. However, there is no doubt in my mind that if I had ignored the chomp, chomp, chomp, it would have rapidly progressed into a problem such as major mouthing.

If you want to build a successful performance career, train yourself to pay attention to the seemingly insignificant details. This is what separates great dog and handler teams from mediocre ones. Don't allow yourself to be lulled into a delusional state by thinking that the problem will miraculously go away on its own.

A few years ago Stephen King, the famous mystery writer, made a comparison between writing and dandelions. The analogy stuck with me and how, if tweaked just a little, it perfectly defined dog training problems. What could the two possibly have in common, you ask? If you have one dandelion growing in your lawn, it doesn't seem like a big deal. After all, look at the enormous expanse of green lawn compared to that one little dandelion. However, if you fail to immediately root out that dandelion, the next day there will be two dandelions growing in your lawn. A week later you will wake up to find your lawn is a sea of yellow dandelions. Training problems, like dandelions, creep up and get out of control in a big hurry unless you deal with the situation immediately.

A young English Cocker perfecting his down-stay.

Be demanding. Be objective. Don't ignore the small details.

If a dog has always been eager and enthusiastic about working and suddenly one day his attitude plummets, that is a pretty good indication that something unrelated to training is going on, such as an injury or illness. Dogs that are raised with a good attitude and a strong desire to work do not decide overnight to stop working.

On the other hand, if your two-year-old dog has always had a wimpy, I-can't-do-it attitude, where do you think he got that attitude? One lady who trained with me couldn't figure out why her two-year-old competition dog "suddenly" developed a slow response to her commands. In reality the dog did not develop this attitude overnight. Over a period of time the woman had allowed him to develop a habit of slow response and the dog took advantage of the situation.

BE OBJECTIVE

You must be consistently objective about your puppy's progress and performance. Equally important, you need to remain objective and demanding as your dog matures and is involved in a competitive career. For example, is your two-year-old Greyhound still enthusiastic, or is he getting lazy? Is your three-year-old retriever beginning to enter water sluggishly? Is your agility dog out of control on the course, or your obedience dog slowing down on his recalls or retrieves?

I repeat, if you want to succeed in any competitive canine environment, you must be both demanding and objective regarding your puppy's training. Of course, it goes without saying that your level of demand should be proportional to his age and physical and mental capabilities. Demanding should never be interpreted as treating the puppy mean or harshly. You are teaching the puppy to respond in a particular fashion each and every time you give a command until that action becomes habit for him. Never put your puppy in a position where he can develop bad habits such as sour attitude, disrespect, slow retrieves, sloppy sits, leisurely recalls, and so on.

Once your puppy masters a behavior, it must be maintained. You cannot take the behavior for granted because "he already knows it." You must continue reinforcing the behaviors in a fun and humane manner.

NO EXCUSES

Always be objective about what you or your puppy are doing in a training situation. For example, if you tell your puppy to come but he ignores you and decides to sniff a pile of leaves, don't pretend he couldn't hear. Avoid the habit of making excuses for your puppy. Don't say, "Oh, the wind was blowing so he couldn't hear me." We all know a dog's hearing is far superior to a human's. If you make excuses for his inattentiveness outside the ring, you will constantly struggle to succeed inside the ring because you lack the open-mindedness to accept the problem and remedy it. Be objective. Fix that problem today.

Equally important, do not avoid a situation because you fear the possibility that your puppy might not respond. For example, never avoid calling your puppy or telling him "down" because you think he is not going to pay attention and you do not want to confront the problem. The situation will not magically improve in competition. Deal with that problem today!

Success is measured in individual triumphs and accomplishments.

MAINTAIN TRUST AND RESPECT

The bottom line: If you want your puppy to become a well-adjusted, happy, motivated adult dog, eager and willing to perform inside and outside the ring, you must first establish mutual trust and respect in your day-to-day life. Second, your dog must have a thorough understanding of what you expect from him, both in training and in a competitive situation. This mutual trust and respect, coupled with the good training, is what will enable him to excel.

Dogs have the uncanny ability to teach us humility. They reduce our world to basics. There is a winner at every show. Chances are it will not always be you. Success, however, is not measured by who brings home the rosettes. It is measured in individual triumphs and accomplishments between you and your dog. If a dog that has been particularly difficult to train scores 185 in the obedience ring, you should feel a sense of accomplishment. Do not give a second thought to the naysayers outside the ring who ask, "What happened with him?" They have no idea of the trials and tribulations you endured during training, and no concept of how many hours you invested in order to overcome various training problems.

Bobbie Anderson with her German Shepherd, Von Berguntahl Elite, CDX, take High in Trial.

THE BEGINNING, NOT THE END

Remember: You are not training for today; you are training for three years down the road when you will be competing for a Utility, Masters Agility, or Tracking Dog Excellent title. If you want 85 percent attention from your dog in competition, then demand 200 percent attention in training.

I cannot deny that there are plenty of heartaches and disappointments in the quest for success. Yet, whenever I need a reason to smile, I need only to look at my next up-and-coming superstars. They restore my spirit and hope, and never fail to fulfill me. I know success will always be a part of our future. I trust that it will be your destiny as well, as you use these building blocks to shape and motivate your next competition star.

WHAT YOU SAY IS WHAT YOU GET

To improve your training sessions as well as your attitude, learn to monitor your speech patterns. How many times a day do you use a negative? Are you a complainer? Do you self-sabotage? Censor your speech and toss the following words from your vocabulary:

• *Can't* — A tiny word that does much harm. Remember what Henry Ford said: "If you think you can do something, you're right. If you think you can't do it, you're still right." Rather than say, "I can't get my dog to play," say, "I will work diligently to help my dog learn to play."

• *Never* — "I never have time to train my dogs." Be positive. Make time. Say, "I will train my dogs today."

• *Won't* — Another word that can sabotage your efforts. Think "will" instead of "won't." "I won't be nervous" becomes "I will be relaxed."

• *If* — Using "if" shows a lack of self-confidence. Say "*When* I get my OTCH," or "when I go High in Trial."

For Further Information

ASSOCIATIONS

Agility Association of Canada
www.aac.ca

AKC Breeder Referral Service
900-407-7877

American Canine Sports Medicine Association
(ACSMA)
P.O. Box 82433
Baton Rouge, LA 70884
E-mail: acsma@acsma.com
www.acsma.org

American College of Veterinary Nutrition
Department of Large Animal Clinical Sciences
Virginia-Maryland Regional College of
    Veterinary Medicine
Blacksburg, VA 24061-0442
540-231-3956
E-mail: idascani@vt.edu
www.acvn.org

American Kennel Club (AKC)
Customer Service Department
5580 Centerview Drive
Raleigh, NC 27606-3390
919-233-9767
E-mail: info@akc.org
www.akc.org

American Rare Breed Association
9921 Frank Tippett Road
Cheltenham, MD 20623
301-868-5719
E-mail: info@arba.org
www.arba.org

American Sighthound Field Association (ASFA)
www.asfa.org

Canadian Kennel Club (CKC)
89 Skyway Avenue, Suite 100
Etobicoke, ON, Canada M9W 6R4
800-250-8040
416-675-5511
E-mail: information@ckc.ca
www.ckc.ca

Canine Eye Registration Foundation (CERF)
1248 Lynn Hall
Purdue University
West Lafayette, IN 47907
765-494-8179
www.vet.purdue.edu/~yshen/cerf.html

Continental Kennel Club, Inc.
P.O. Box 908
Walker, LA 70785
800-952-3376
E-mail: ckc@ckcusa.com
www.ckcusa.com

International Federation of Sled Dog Sports
Sally O'Sullivan Bair / Secretary General
3381 Troy Brett Trail
Duluth, MN 55803
218-525-4012
E-mail: sallybair@msn.com

International Sheep Dog Society
Clifton House
4a Goldington Road
Bedford
MK403NF
United Kingdom
44(12)34352672
E-mail: office@intersheepdogsoc.org.uk

LV/DVG (all breed Schutzhund)
c/o Sandi Purdy
2101 S. Westmoreland Road
Red Oak, TX 75154
972-617-2988
E-mail: Spurdy5718@aol.com
www.dvgamerica.com

National Greyhound Association Registry (NGA)
P.O. Box 543
Abilene, KS 67410
785-263-4660
E-mail: nga@jc.net

National Kennel Club
255 Indian Ridge Road
P.O. Box 331
Blaine, TN 37709
865-932-9680
E-mail: dmorga22@bellsouth.net
www.nationalkennelclub.com

North American Dog Agility Council
11550 S. Hwy 3
Cataldo, ID 83810
E-mail: nadack9@aol.com
www.nadac.com

North American Flyball Association, Inc.
1400 W. Devon Avenue, #512
Chicago, IL 60660
309-688-9840
E-mail: flyball@flyball.org
www.flyball.org

Orthopedic Foundation for Animals (OFA)
2300 E. Nifong Blvd.
Columbia, MO 65201-3856
573-442-0418
E-mail: ofa@offa.org
www.offa.org

Owner Handlers' Association
c/o Rose Robischon
914-374-2708
E-mail: ur6146@exmail.usma.army.mil

Professional Handlers' Association, Inc.
17017 Norbrook Drive
Olney, MD 20832
301-924-0089

Professional Kennel Club
P.O. Box 8338
Evansville, IN 47716-8338
800-238-5009
www.prohound.com

State Kennel Club (SKC)
P.O. Box 230
Hattiesburg, MS 39403
601-583-8345
E-mail: skc@netdoor.com

The Kennel Club
1 Clarges Street
London, England
W1J8AB
44(870) 6066750
www.the-kennel-club.org.uk/crufts

United States Dog Agility Association
P.O. Box 850955
Richardson, TX 75085-0955
972-487-2200
E-mail: info@usdaa.com
www.usdaa.com

UC Davis Veterinary Genetics Laboratory
    (for DNA testing)
530-752-2211
University of California
Davis, CA 95616-8744
E-mail: dogdna@vgl.ucdavis.edu
www.vgl.ucdavis.edu/research/canine

United Kennel Club, Inc.
100 E. Kilgore Road
Kalamazoo, MI 49002-5584
616-343-9020
www.ukcdogs.com

About the Authors

Bobbie Anderson is a successful exhibitor, trainer, and former AKC obedience judge whose involvement in the sport began in 1970 with a miniature Schnauzer. Anderson has since become one of the foremost ranking dog trainers in the country. She has put over seventy AKC titles on dogs, including five Obedience Trial Championships, three Utility Dog Excellent, twelve Utility Dog, and seven Tracking Dog titles, and over eight-five High in Trial wins. She accomplished this with multiple breeds including Shelties, English Cockers, German Shepherds and Border Collies.

The owner and instructor of Eugene Obedience Training in Eugene, Oregon, since 1978, Anderson teaches all levels of competition obedience. Her successes have garnered her a loyal and devoted following of students with titles at all levels.

Tracy J. Libby is an award-winning freelance writer whose work has appeared in numerous publications including the *AKC Gazette, You and Your Dog, Your Cat, Oregon Magazine, Travelog,* and *Family Motor Coaching.* She is a member of the Dog Writers' Association of America and a recipient of the Elsworth S. Howell award for distinguished dog writing. She actively shows Australian Shepherds in both obedience and conformation. Libby is also a resident of Oregon.

YOU'LL WANT TO READ THESE, TOO . . .

How to Raise a Puppy You Can Live With
Clarice Rutherford and David H. Neil
Our classic best-seller, this book deals with raising a puppy from birth to one year, including the all-important four- to-eight-week socialization period during which the breeder shapes the puppy's behavior, and the developmental periods that are critical for the new owner to understand. Make the most of your next puppy. Read this book!
ISBN 1-57779-022-7

The New Guide to Better Behavior in Dogs
William Campbell
A dog trainer and behaviorist looks at how dogs communicate, how to understand your dog better, and how to prevent problem behaviors from developing. A standard work on basic dog behavior as it relates to training.
ISBN 1-57779-018-9

Successful Obedience Handling
Barbara Handler
Improve your obedience scores by improving your own handling skills. This book tells you what to expect, what you can and cannot do at a trial, and explains the finer points of handling that make the difference between an average and a winning score. A must for obedience competitors at any level.
ISBN 0-931866-51-0

Beyond Basic Dog Training—The Workbook
Diane Bauman et al.
A practical workbook with games, challenges, puzzles and more to stimulate creativity and prevent boredom while practicing obedience routines. A supplement to Bauman's popular training manual.
ISBN 0-931866-74-X

Scent: Training to Track, Search and Rescue
Milo Pearsall and Hugo Verbruggen
Pearsall was one of the early leaders in obedience training and the author of numerous books on the subject. Here he teams up with a medical doctor to examine the dog's unique ability to scent, how dog's follow a track, and how to use that understanding when training in the field. Complete series of lessons for training a dog to track, search, or rescue, too. An important work all tracking enthusiasts should read.
ISBN 0-931866-11-1

Puppy Parenting
Gail Clark
In order to have a mentally sound dog, you need to parent the puppy effectively. That starts with selecting the right puppy for your needs, and shaping his psyche carefully as he grows.
ISBN 1-57779-012-X

The Mentally Sound Dog
Gail Clark
For people who encounter behavior problems with their dog, Clark draws on her vast experience in resolving them.
Read this book—you'll be glad you did!
ISBN 0-931866-67-7

These and other fine Alpine Blue Ribbon titles are available at your local bookseller or pet supply outlet, or you may order direct from the publisher at 1-800-777-7257 or by writing to Alpine Publications, P.O. Box 7027, Loveland, CO 80537.

For latest information and prices, check our web site: www.alpinepub.com